# BACK FROM THE BRINK

### THE FIGHT TO SAVE OUR ENDANGERED BIRDS

To Mum and Dad

# BACK FROM THE BRINK

## THE FIGHT TO SAVE OUR ENDANGERED BIRDS

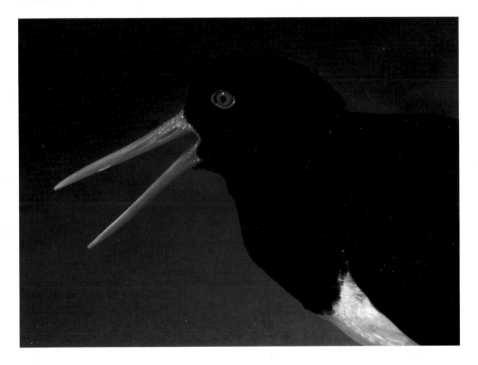

## GERARD HUTCHING

PENGUIN BOOKS

PENGUIN BOOKS
Published by the Penguin Group
Penguin Group (NZ), cnr Airborne and Rosedale Roads, Albany,
Auckland 1310, New Zealand
Penguin Books Ltd, 80 Strand, London, WC2R 0RL, England
Penguin Group (USA) Inc., 375 Hudson Street, New York, NY 10014, United States
Penguin Group (Australia), 250 Camberwell Road, Camberwell,
Victoria 3124, Australia
Penguin Books Canada Ltd, 10 Alcorn Avenue, Toronto,
Ontario, Canada M4V 3B2
Penguin Books (South Africa) (Pty) Ltd, 24 Sturdee Avenue, Rosebank,
Johannesburg 2196, South Africa
Penguin Books India (P) Ltd, 11, Community Centre, Panchsheel Park,
New Delhi 110 017, India
Penguin Ireland Ltd, 25 St Stephen's Green, Dublin 2, Ireland
Penguin Books Ltd, Registered Offices: 80 Strand, London, WC2R 0RL, England

First published by Penguin Group (NZ), 2004
1 3 5 7 9 10 8 6 4 2

Copyright © text Gerard Hutching, 2004
Copyright © photographs individual photographers

The right of Gerard Hutching to be identified as the author of this work in terms of
section 96 of the Copyright Act 1994 is hereby asserted.

Designed by Nick Turzynski
Printed by Condor Production, Hong Kong

ISBN 0 14 301948 1
A catalogue record for this book is available
from the National Library of New Zealand.

www.penguin.co.nz

# Contents

# Introduction

I often wonder what happened to Tawbert. One of the last of the Fiordland kakapo ever to be seen, in the summer of 1986 Tawbert clung to life at about 1000 metres altitude in the Transit Valley, a typically steep-sided basin gouged out of the resistant rock by glaciers. Tawbert was a surviving remnant of the Fiordland kakapo population. After the Wildlife Service launched its 'last chance to save the kakapo' campaign in 1974, it discovered 18 birds in remote mountainous retreats during the 1970s, all of which were males. By 1986 there were only six left.

During our stay in the Transit Valley, Tawbert proved elusive. Our goal was to track him down by listening to him 'booming', the male kakapo's unique signal to any females in the vicinity that he is ready to breed. But that year he had worked out that it would not be a good year for breeding, that there would not be sufficient food to raise a demanding kakapo fledgling or two. In the end, modern technology

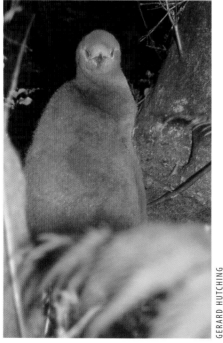

GERARD HUTCHING

On the mainland the yellow-eyed penguin faces myriad threats but this chick, photographed on a secure island, has better chances of survival.

GERARD HUTCHING

The gregarious kaka was once widespread. Efforts by DOC to establish mainland islands have benefited this forest relative of the kea.

■ The kea, or alpine parrot, is a hardy bird and appears to be holding its own, although a century of persecution by farmers has drastically reduced its numbers. It is now fully protected.

helped us trace him. Like all Fiordland kakapo, he had a transmitter strapped to his back and, by following beeps rather than booms, we finally found him after an exhausting day of bashing through subalpine scrub. After some quick measurements and a photo opportunity, we left the placid giant parrot to find a log to hide under and continue his presumably solitary existence.

That was the last anyone saw of Tawbert; it is a fair assumption that he is now dead, because most of the 18 kakapo found in Fiordland were believed to be birds in their dotage. That said, however, the last surviving Fiordland kakapo, Richard Henry, is still alive and breeding, almost 30 years after being plucked from alpine obscurity.

If the story of those remaining Fiordland kakapo is a tragedy, then the kakapo tale since then is one of triumph, culminating in the breakthrough breeding year of 2002. The thread running through a number of the stories in this book is that without human intervention extinction would have occurred. That is especially so in the case of the black robin, the black stilt and the kakapo, which were undoubtedly heading down the road to oblivion 20 years ago. Birds like the Chatham Island oystercatcher would likely have struggled on in low numbers, but a helping human hand has boosted their population in recent years.

Therefore, this is an unashamedly good-news book. The bad news is that especially on mainland New Zealand native species are still on a downward spiral. It is no coincidence that most of the success stories have occurred on islands where predators can be eradicated. On the mainland it is not so easy. The blue duck, kaka, brown kiwi, brown teal, kokako, mohua, orange-fronted parakeet and wrybill are just a few of the birds under threat. While conservation managers have shown that birds can thrive on 'mainland islands', what of those unfortunate enough to live outside these scattered specially protected areas? Furthermore, islands, whether mainland or natural, are no answer to species like the blue duck which needs long stretches of swift-flowing rivers in which to survive, or birds of specialised habitats such as the wrybill which has adapted to life alongside South Island braided rivers.

In the medium to long term, new, smart techniques to protect these species from predators will have to be found. New Zealanders have shown a remarkable ability to fashion innovative solutions to conservation problems: removing cats, rats and possums from any number of islands is just one example. Professional conservationists – staff from the Department of Conservation (DOC), Landcare Research and the universities – have played a leading role in these bold undertakings. However, the professional effort has always depended on public support. One of the outstanding features of contemporary political life in New Zealand has been the broad, cross-party backing for conservation. And that concern goes beyond the political level. Ordinary people today are more involved than ever in grassroots attempts to restore forests, wetlands or high-country tussocklands. Whether it is trying to control possums in an Eastbourne forest, or cats in the Waitakeres, conservation-minded citizens have taken matters into their own hands – and in many cases succeeded.

However, without reliable information about the status of species, conservation managers do not know where to put scarce resources. Scientists have therefore identified the species that are at risk of extinction, and the level and nature of that risk. As a result they have divided species into the following five categories, according to level of risk: species which are nationally critical, nationally endangered, nationally vulnerable, in serious decline and in gradual decline. Of the five categories, the first three comprise birds with the most immediate, pressing needs.

A species that is **nationally critical** is defined as one belonging to a very small population or which has a very high predicted decline. The total population size is less than 250 mature individuals and the species is predicted to decline to less than 80 per cent of the total population in the next 10 years. **Nationally endangered** species have small populations of between 250 and 1000 mature individuals, and

**nationally vulnerable** birds number between 1000 and 5000. Other factors are important as well, such as the area of habitat that the survivors live in, and how many separate populations there are.

According to these criteria, New Zealand birds most at risk have been placed into one or other of those three categories.

| Nationally critical | Nationally endangered | Nationally vulnerable |
| --- | --- | --- |
| Australasian crested grebe | Australasian bittern | Black-browed mollymawk |
| Black robin | Blue duck | Blue penguin |
| Black stilt | Chatham Island tomtit | Caspian tern |
| Brown teal | Chatham Island tui | Northern royal albatross |
| Campbell Island teal | Chatham petrel | Rock wren |
| Chatham Island oystercatcher | Erect-crested penguin | Stewart Island shag |
| Codfish Island fernbird | Falcon | Wrybill |
| Common noddy | Forbes parakeet | Yellow-eyed penguin |
| Fairy tern | Hutton's shearwater | |
| Kakapo | Kaka (North and South Island) | |
| Kermadec storm petrel | Kea | |
| Kotuku (white heron) | Kermadec petrel | |
| Masked (blue-faced) booby | Kokako (North Island) | |
| New Zealand dotterel (southern subspecies) | Reef heron | |
| Orange-fronted parakeet | Saddleback (South Island) | |
| Parea | Stewart Island fernbird | |
| Rowi | Stewart Island robin | |
| Shore plover | Weka (North Island and Stewart Island) | |
| South Georgian diving petrel | Yellowhead | |
| Taiko (Chatham Island) | | |
| Takahe | | |
| White tern | | |

Fortunately, conservation has come a long way since the days when collectors would compete to be the one to shoot the last of a species. Today the race is on to rescue remaining survivors; the following stories provide proof, in some instances at least, that the race is being hard fought, if not yet won.

# *I* South Island
# Saddleback
*Resilient ground dweller of the south*

| | |
|---|---|
| Scientific name | *Philesturnus carunculatus carunculatus* |
| Popular names | tieke, jackbird |
| Conservation status | nationally endangered |
| Population | 700+ (in 2003) |
| Where found | Big, Kaimohu, North, Kundy, Betsy, Motunui, Jacky Lee, Putauhinu, Pohowaitai and Ulva islands (all surrounding Stewart Island); Breaksea, Passage and Erin islands (Fiordland); Motuara Island (Marlborough Sounds) |
| Lifespan | up to 17 years |
| Size | 80 g (male), 70 g (female); 25 cm |
| Breeding | August–May; most breed the year following hatching |
| Nest sites | tree holes, dense scrub, close to the ground |
| Clutch size | 1–4 eggs; pairs frequently re-nest if time allows in the season |
| Feeding | on and off the ground: caterpillars, spiders, beetles, aphids, wetas, worms, bush cockroaches, moths; saddlebacks are known for their lively feeding habits and attract other birds to feed on disturbed insects |
| Behaviour | poor fliers, their preference is to bound from branch to branch; inquisitive and territorial |

ig South Cape, 1964: a place and a time that marked a sea change in the approach to species conservation in New Zealand. A small island off the south-west coast of Stewart Island, Big South Cape had long been a traditional muttonbirding island, from where local Rakiura Maori harvested plump sooty shearwaters each year between April and May. It was considered a remarkable island for its abundant bird life: bellbirds, tui, kaka, parakeets, robins, fernbirds, moreporks and fantails filled the air with birdsong. And then there were the three bird species found only on the island: the Stewart Island snipe, Stead's bush wren (nicknamed the thumb bird because of its small size) and the South Island saddleback.

Today New Zealand has only two native land mammals, the long-tailed and lesser short-tailed bat, but until 1964 there was a third species, the greater short-tailed bat, which found refuge on the island.

Just as most of New Zealand and its islands had been overrun by predators, so the rats finally reached Big South Cape in August 1962. Ship rats made their way ashore from the muttonbirders' boats and over several seasons established themselves. Their numbers gradually built up until suddenly in 1964 the rat population exploded. By the time the Wildlife Service was alerted to the problem, many of the birds had disappeared or were in low numbers. The bat was one of the first species to go. It was five months before Don Merton and Brian Bell could mount a winter expedition to the island (in the days before helicopters were routinely used for such work). Don Merton explains that at the time some biologists were still not convinced that predators posed a significant threat. Trained in Europe or North America, these scientists regarded predators as a natural part of the ecosystem and maintained that extinctions in New Zealand had been caused by habitat destruction, not predators. 'My colleagues and I weren't convinced. Then the Big South Cape invasion occurred, which not only clinched the argument, but changed forever the way we perceived, protected and managed our living heritage,' says Merton.

Coincidentally, in 1963, Merton and two colleagues, John Kendrick and Ian Atkinson, had been experimenting with catching North Island saddlebacks on Hen Island, near Whangarei, and had refined the technique of capturing them in fine mist nets. With the benefit of this knowledge, they now applied the same method to capturing the saddleback, snipe and Stead's bush wren. Unfortunately they caught only two snipe, which both died before they could be transferred to another island. The team managed to capture nine of the tiny wrens which were ferried across to the safety of rat-free Kaimohu Island. Gradually they died, with a single bird holding on until 1972 when the species was declared extinct. By comparison to these two species, the saddleback proved to be more robust. In all, 36 were taken

DON MERTON

■ The South Island saddleback differs from the North Island subspecies in having smaller wattles and no gold band at the top of the chestnut-coloured saddle.

and relocated to nearby Kaimohu and Big islands (also without rats). The adaptable, ground-dwelling birds prospered on the islands, and as their numbers built up they were distributed among other neighbouring islands, most less than 100 hectares in size.

Once Norway rats were eradicated from Breaksea Island (170 hectares) in Fiordland, 60 saddlebacks were reintroduced there in 1992, marking the furthest distance the birds had been moved from the Stewart Island region. Other releases followed: Motuara Island (59 hectares) in the Marlborough Sounds; Pohowaitai Island (39 hectares) off Stewart Island; Ulva Island (269 hectares) in Paterson Inlet, Stewart Island; Passage Island (176 hectares) in Fiordland; and Erin Island (67 hectares) in Lake Te Anau, Fiordland. From an initial population of just 36, South Island saddleback numbers have increased to more than 700 – a textbook success story. They are now established on 10 islands. In 1971 the International Union for the Conservation of Nature removed the saddleback from its endangered list, the only bird at that stage to have been saved by human intervention.

Despite the fact that the rat invasion had been so catastrophic to the island's wildlife, it had a galvanising effect on people working in conservation, as Don Merton explains, 'The tragedy of Big South Cape was a timely and valuable lesson for us. It convinced even the most sceptical that predators could induce ecological collapse and extinctions. But it also had a massive, enduring impact because it shaped the way we developed policies about conservation and put them into practice.'

# 2 Black Robin

## *Fearless survivor of the Chathams*

| | |
|---|---|
| Scientific name | *Petroica traversi* |
| Popular name | black robin |
| Conservation status | protected nationally critical endemic |
| Population | 200+ (in 2004) |
| Where found | Mangere, South East and Pitt islands (part of the Chathams group) |
| Lifespan | up to 13 years |
| Size | 25 g (male), 22 g (female); 15 cm |
| Breeding | October–November; most breed at 2 years of age |
| Nest sites | prefers cavities in trees and vine tangles, 1–6 m off the ground |
| Clutch size | 1–3 eggs; pairs frequently re-nest if time allows in the season |
| Feeding | on and off the ground: caterpillars, spiders, beetles, aphids, wetas, worms, bush cockroaches, moths |
| Behaviour | strongly territorial during breeding; female builds nest and incubates; both adults feed young; generally retain the same partner and territory from year to year |

Few conservation rescue stories have captured the public imagination anywhere in the world like that of the Chatham Island black robin. In 1980, with only five birds left and only one breeding pair, the robin came within a whisker of extinction. However, by dint of sheer effort and imaginative risk-taking, conservation legend Don Merton and his team coaxed the species back from the brink. Using a close relative, the Chatham Island tomtit, as foster parents, more robin chicks were hatched and raised than would have been possible if it had been left to the robins themselves. Today, the matriarch of the species, Old Blue, is celebrated in people's memories, in awards for conservation services and in the birds that are her legacy. By 2004 that legacy numbered around 200 plus. The tale of how the robin was rescued is well documented; less well known is what happened after the species was considered 'safe', and the difficult management decisions that had to be taken during the 1990s.

To recap, the black robin was once widespread throughout the islands of the Chathams group, 860 kilometres east of New Zealand, but by the time ornithologist Henry Travers arrived in 1871, it was present only on Mangere (113 hectares) and 200-metre-high Little Mangere (22 hectares) islands, separated by just a few hundred metres. 'I found this bird at Mangare [*sic*], where it is not uncommon,' he wrote. 'It is very fearless, possessing in other respects the habits of *Petroica albifrons* [as the South Island robin was known at the time].' This endearing feature, and the

DON MERTON

■ 'Like an aircraft carrier moored in the Roaring Forties' – an apt description of Little Mangere Island, last refuge of the black robin.

bird's poor ability to fly, meant it was easy prey for introduced cats and rats.

Little was heard of the robin again until 1937, when two Auckland University students, Charles Fleming and Graham Turbott, and local schoolteacher Allan Wotherspoon, climbed the daunting heights of Little Mangere to search for the tiny bird. They had failed to find any on Mangere Island; little wonder, as cats had been let loose there in the latter decades of the nineteenth century. The island was also extensively burned for grazing, inflicting further casualties on the wildlife. Miraculously, Little Mangere had been spared predators, and the party estimated there were between 20 and 35 pairs of robins still surviving on the minute island, hardly larger than a rock stack.

Conservation was then in its infancy and the fate of the black robin was largely ignored until the 1970s when dedicated Wildlife Service staff such as Brian Bell and Don Merton drew attention to the bird's plight. During centuries of isolation the population had fluctuated, possibly down to single figures; certainly the degree of inbreeding points to this. By 1976 there were just seven birds. Sooty shearwaters, burrowing by the thousands on the five hectares of scrub at the summit where the robins lived, helped degrade the vegetation. More precious forest was cleared for a helicopter landing pad. If nothing was done, the species would soon become extinct.

Precious opportunities had already been lost. In 1972 there were still more than 20 robins left, but while researchers debated what to do, the population plummeted. Don Merton advocated that the survivors should be shifted to adjoining Mangere.

Already the ground had been prepared for a rescue attempt. On Mangere, the Wildlife Service, itself a tiny group of specialists working on desperately small budgets, had planted 120,000 cuttings of leathery, salt-resistant Chatham Island ake ake (*Olearia traversi*) seedlings, the type of forest the robin was thought to favour. Rabbits had died out, Pitt Islanders shot the last of the cats, and grazing animals were removed. Crossing the surging ocean between Mangere and Little Mangere islands in 1976, the rescue team climbed up near-vertical rocks to the summit, captured their valuable cargo and carried them back down in specially designed backpack transfer boxes. No helicopters existed on the Chathams to help them; the crayfish industry had gone from boom to bust and the helicopters had returned to the mainland.

The bold decision to transfer the robins was vindicated in the next few years, since more chicks began to survive to breeding age again. However, despite the increase in chicks, more birds were dying than being hatched. By 1980 the population was down to five with the only breeding female being Old Blue. Again, something drastic had to be done.

DON MERTON

■ Wildlife scientists scale steep rocks to the summit of Little Mangere Island.

DON MERTON

■ A black robin chick expectantly awaits a meal from a tomtit. By the late 1980s the black robins could go it alone without the aid of the tomtits.

Recalling his childhood experiments with his grandmother's canary when he used to induce it to raise goldfinch chicks, Don Merton placed black robin eggs in a Chatham Island warbler (*Gerygone albofrontata*) nest, hoping they would be fostered. They were, but the first chick died of starvation after 10 days when the warblers appeared to lose interest in feeding it. Swiftly the second chick was returned to Old Blue's nest where it was successfully raised.

Plainly, the warbler was not an ideal foster parent. The next likely candidate – the Chatham Island tomtit – no longer lived on Mangere but on nearby South East (Rangatira) Island. As a precaution against competition for food and space in the small forest remnant, the tomtits had been removed from Mangere. A robin egg was taken from Mangere to South East and trialled in a tomtit nest during the 1980–81 season. This proved that the tomtit could raise the robin through to the fledgling stage and soon tomtits were pressed into service as foster parents.

Up until 1983 robin chicks were returned to Mangere, but in that year it was decided to establish a new population of robins on South East, a much larger island offering better long-term prospects for the species. So it proved, and each year numbers of robins increased on both islands. However, one complication tempered the optimism of Don Merton and his colleagues. Two significant changes in robin behaviour indicated that there was a mal-imprinting problem. Some robins reared by tomtits through to the fledgling stage now acted as though they were tomtits. A small number of fostered female robins selected tomtit partners, one pair even producing hybrid offspring. At one stage robin song – vital for attracting female mates – was almost extinguished. The solution to this mal-imprinting was to take the robin chicks out of the tomtit nests a few days before they were due to fledge, and to place them back in a robin's nest. Fortunately the robin adults accepted the newcomers, raising them to maturity and passing on robin characteristics to the fledglings.

As if this unexpected problem was not enough, there were others which were more run of the mill: storms and rock falls which obliterated nests; petrels which tumbled through forest canopies and broke eggs; avian disease which killed adults and chicks. Seasonal nest mite infestations also made life uncomfortable both for birds and humans.

By 1989, though, with the population at a relatively healthy 99, it was felt that the robins could just about fend for themselves. There were still some lingering concerns, however, that they might not yet be out of the woods. All the birds were descended from a single female, Old Blue – so the robin gene pool was likely to be extremely limited – and in such a small population interbreeding between parents and siblings had been common. They also had the odd habit of occasionally laying eggs on the rim of the nest rather than right into it.

Rather than continue the hands-on management of the 1980s, a team under Euan Kennedy started an intensive three-year monitoring programme without interfering in the birds' breeding. Euan's involvement in the black robin story began in winter 1978 when he first visited Mangere as a volunteer to plant ake ake trees. He became part of the team working on the robin, not to mention other species such as the Chatham petrel and shore plover. A dedicated conservationist, he had been recruited into the Wildlife Service in the mid-1970s after completing an honours degree in German literature. His was an unusual background to have for work in a government agency otherwise dominated by trainees not long out of school, wildlife officers who had come through the cadet system, and a smattering of wildlife scientists.

Known for his forthright views, Kennedy was regarded as a person who saw beyond the immediate goal of saving species. Intolerant of bureaucrats and others who stood in the way of conservation, he was a staunch advocate of more professional management of wildlife, and for better conservation funding. By 1990, having worked with the robin for many years, he knew as much as anyone – bar perhaps Don Merton – about managing the species, although he is quick to point

# Strength through **adversity**

The Chatham Island black robin, arguably the world's most inbred bird, is thriving in spite of its lack of genetic diversity. Recent 'minisatellite' DNA profiling has revealed that the 200-strong population is virtually identical, except for the differences between males and females. The finding was not totally unexpected, since all black robins are descended from a single pair.

On any measure, the robins are prospering. In fact, compared to their mainland cousin the bush robin (*Petroica australis australis*), they show a higher percentage of nestlings fledged (70.3 per cent compared to 42 per cent) and a higher percentage of survival to the first year (75.6 per cent against 28.2 per cent). However, the bush robin's higher mortality can be accounted for by the presence of predators on the mainland, whereas the black robin islands are free of stoats, cats and rats.

Don Merton believes the difficult living conditions the robins have experienced over the last few hundred years have stood them in good stead. 'The birds have been able to tolerate a wide range of climatic conditions. They went through a genetic bottleneck for 100 years on Little Mangere – in effect on the deck of an aircraft carrier moored in the Roaring Forties – then the ultimate bottleneck when they were down to at the most four or five breeding pairs over a 10-year period. I believe all that has left them much better able to withstand adversity,' says Merton.

Professor David Lambert and his research group from the Department of Ecology at Massey University, who carried out the DNA analyses, is now to investigate another region of the black robin genome – the major histocompatibility complex (MHC), which is the basis of individuals' immunological response to invading pathogens.

Professor Lambert says it is interesting to compare the black robins with cheetahs, which have been shown to exhibit reproduction and viability problems, possibly related to their lack of genetic variation. 'In contrast to cheetahs, robins are increasing in numbers, and the proportion of chicks fledged is very high by comparison with mainland robins. History has done something for the robin, in that over a long period of time, genes which were deleterious to robins were eliminated because the population size was so small,' he says.

DON MERTON

■ A trusting Chatham Island tomtit watches as Don Merton shifts a foster nest, South East Island, 1987.

out that he lacks Merton's intuitive knowledge of bird behaviour. However, he knew the Chathams well, and by 1998 had become the longest-serving member of the robin team. Based in Christchurch, he was placed in charge of key wildlife programmes in the Chathams, and took a particular interest in the black robin.

Over the three years from 1990, robin numbers increased to one hundred and twenty. But now that the species was considered out of the danger zone, fewer resources were being directed towards it. Coupled with general budget cuts in the

■ 'Jimmy' was named after Jimmy Preece of the Pitt Island farming family. The Preece family have recently placed a forested area of their property into a reserve into which black robins have been released.

■ The Chatham Island tomtit played a crucial role in rescuing the robin by hatching robin eggs. Ironically the tomtit is itself a rare bird, numbering in the several hundreds.

Department of Conservation (DOC), the pressure mounted on robin minders to scale the monitoring programme back. Up to that point, says Kennedy, almost every robin's parentage could be accounted for. But in the 1993–94 season there came a sharp reminder that it might be too soon to bring monitoring to a halt. Returning to Mangere in late spring, observers saw three unfamiliar and unbanded robins. Clearly, budget cuts and skills shortages had resulted in serious monitoring lapses in previous years. Even more unsettling, one of the robins was courtship feeding a tomtit female – a signal that mating had occurred or was about to. Recalls Kennedy: 'It was shattering to find a male black robin paired with a female tomtit. During intensive management, misbehaving birds – all of them fostered female robins – had been separated from their partners. After we removed these birds from South East and kept a close eye on the surviving tomtit-raised females, the risk of cross-breeding was considered to have passed.'

A debate ensued about what to do. Destroy the pair or monitor them and their newly hatched chicks, now dubbed 'robotits'? Kennedy was for the latter course, reasoning that they should wait to see if the robotits were fertile or not. If they proved infertile, fears about cross-breeding or other such events in the future would fade. Others argued that no chances should be taken and they should be destroyed immediately.

The latter viewpoint won the day; staff on the island were asked to destroy the errant pair. But meanwhile back in Wellington the then minister of conservation, Denis Marshall, was having second thoughts about the decision following persuasive plea bargaining by opponents. They insisted cross-breeding was a natural evolutionary occurrence and that humans had no right to interfere in the process.

It was a moment of high drama. Staff had just arrived in the nesting territory of the pair when a runner sent from their distant hut intercepted them. The minister had slapped a moratorium on the management of all cross-breeding in native wildlife. He wanted time to review the problem of hybridising in endangered species and the long-established practice of intervening to stop it.

Unaware of how closely they had avoided the death sentence, the robin and his tomtit female raised two 'smudgy' robotits named Tom and Pitt. Kennedy says that, as is common when watching animals closely, people had become fond of them – which made it all the more heart-wrenching when Marshall decided a year later that the birds must be destroyed after all. His reasoning now was that this cross-breeding situation was an unnatural event triggered by human-induced changes to habitat quality and population size. It was early 1995. Again staff were dispatched but this time there was no last-minute reprieve.

But just when many thought the threat of cross-breeding had been resolved, unsettling news arrived. Massey University geneticists had constructed DNA profiles of the dead birds, only to find that the male black robin parent was not a robin at all, but a half robin-half tomtit. This unwelcome surprise confirmed that robotits were fertile. 'I had had my suspicions about the male black robin. It behaved like a tomtit in subtle ways; it seemed to have tomtit elements to its calls. I thought that maybe it was a robin that had been brought up by tomtits somehow,' says Kennedy.

# What's in a **name?**

New Zealand robins are not related to European robins, although they do share their confiding nature, as anyone who has coaxed one down to feed on the forest floor will confirm. It is therefore not difficult to understand why they would have been named after their northern hemisphere counterparts. In fact, they belong to the flycatcher family.

One difference between the real robins and the New Zealand ones is immediately obvious: their colouring. The famous English robin redbreast is a much gaudier character than the New Zealand robins, although the South Island robin has an attractive yellow-white-coloured breast.

On the Chatham Islands, this lack of colour has been taken to extremes in the case of the black robin, a consequence of it being an island species without the ever-present threat of predators. On the mainland, the North and South Island robins are counter-shaded to blend in with the forest, but the black robin has dispensed with this camouflage altogether; nor can it fly for any sustained period.

Plainly this robin had been produced by an earlier, undetected cross-breeding pair; the question now was whether they were still alive and breeding, and if so, where. Before breeding the following season, blood samples were taken from the robins, but nothing was amiss. It was assumed by the opponents of further robin monitoring that the original cross-breeders had died, and (once again) that cross-breeding had ceased to be a problem.

Kennedy was not convinced. The robins had wrong-footed their minders before and he sensed that they might do it again. Towards the end of that breeding season, his colleague Mike Bell, another of DOC's few experienced robin observers, visited Mangere, climbing to a solitary insignificant patch of bush and there found a female black robin brooding three hybrid chicks about to fly from the nest and being assiduously fed by a tomtit. Kennedy now knew who the parents of the robotit were, or at least the identity of the mother. She was Peg, the daughter of a fostered female robin who had mated with tomtits many years before.

Peg proved to be a black robin; she had not been fostered so no mal-imprinting had occurred. That left two possibilities: that the preference to mate with tomtits had been passed down from her mother to her; or that she had been forced to mate

DON MERTON

The Pitt Island aviary in which black robins are housed before release into the Ellen Elizabeth Preece Conservation Covenant, in the hope of establishing a third population . . .

GRAEME TAYLOR

Predator-proof fence surrounding part of the Ellen Elizabeth Preece Conservation Covenant on Pitt Island. Black robins have recently been released here in an effort to establish a third population.

EUAN KENNEDY

■ Like many New Zealand birds, black robins are quite fearless. Without predators to worry them on Little Mangere and South East islands, the robins have thrived; it is a different story on the mainland where robin breeding success is much lower.

EUAN KENNEDYY

with a tomtit because there were not enough male robins to go around. The answer might never be known, though Kennedy believes the latter hypothesis is more likely. The doubt and the incident underline the need to continue closely monitoring the black robins, stresses Kennedy. Yet despite his and others' concerns, the monitoring programme was scaled back dramatically in 2000, though for the meantime it continues as before on Mangere. There were more than 200 birds at the last full population count, but Kennedy rues the fact that 'we'll never again know

■ Euan Kennedy collects robin eggs to 'candle' them. This involves shining a strong torchlight onto the eggs to see whether they are fertile.

just how many there are for sure, and a priceless genealogical record for an entire species has been compromised. But more importantly, we've lost our crucial ability to detect the early stages of problems which might threaten the robin's survival.'

At about this time Kennedy drops out of the black robin story. At present he is analysing the robin monitoring data as a PhD student at Lincoln University, hoping to determine what the birds can tell wildlife specialists elsewhere in the world about the survival prospects of similarly endangered bird species.

After DOC was restructured in 1997, responsibility for the Chatham Islands shifted from Canterbury to Wellington. Inheriting the black robin (and other species) programmes was Hilary Aikman, who acknowledges the weight of expectation attached to the robin's fortunes. 'There is a lot of interest. Sometimes it can be hard to ignore that; it's like something perched on your shoulder. We did a transfer recently and Don Merton and Brian Bell came along and helped. They were thrilled,' she says.

Hilary has a varied background, starting in Wellington Zoo, then briefly attempting a carpentry apprenticeship before working at the DOC wildlife centre at Mt Bruce in the Wairarapa. There she oversaw breeding programmes for endangered species such as the shore plover, black stilt, blue duck and the Campbell Island teal, while studying for a diploma in wildlife management at Otago University.

The decision to stop monitoring the robins was controversial, she agrees, but she does not feel there was sufficient justification to continue. 'It was a recognition first of all of the fact that there were just over 200 birds and secondly there was a huge staff time cost. People needed to be on South East Island for five months and that has a cost to the environment from people through falling through burrows and so on. Hybridisation was only a short-term problem and we have seen no evidence of hybridisation since,' says Aikman.

The chances of the black robin population expanding much beyond its present population on Mangere and South East are slight, simply because there is not sufficient habitat. In assessing other islands to start a new population, Aikman and her team settled on Pitt Island – not an ideal site because there are cats, mice, weka and pigs present. However, a recently protected area on the island, the Ellen Elizabeth Preece covenant, offered a possibility. The Xcluder company has built an exclosure fence around 40 hectares of the 63-hectare reserve which stops weka and cats, though not mice, from entering.

In September 2002, 14 adult black robins were transferred into the reserve. However, high winds proved their undoing, most of them dispersing across the

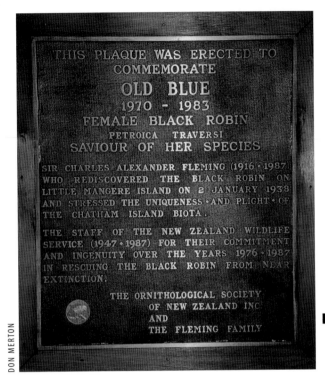

DON MERTON

■ A plaque erected at
Chatham Island airport to
commemorate Old Blue,
the saviour of her species.

island; just one pair established within the covenant area, but outside the exclosure fence. These two did not survive long, and are presumed to have fallen victim to roaming cats. In early 2004 a further 20 were released, of which 10 were still alive by the winter of the same year.

Aikman says that ultimately she would like to see new populations established not just on Pitt Island, but also the main Chatham Island. This will be a move that will not only benefit the robin. Having heard so much about this small, endearing bird that was once the rarest in the world, Chatham Islanders may one day have the opportunity to see them in their own backyards.

## References

'*Black robin recovery plan, 2001–2011*', Department of Conservation, 2001.

Butler, D. and Merton, D., *The Black Robin Story: Saving the World's Most Endangered Bird*, Oxford University Press, 1992.

Kennedy, Euan, *To see or not to see – the cautionary tale of black robin monitoring*.

# 3 Kaki

*Call of the upland wader*

| | |
|---|---|
| Scientific name | *Himantopus novaezelandiae* |
| Popular names | kaki, black stilt |
| Conservation status | protected nationally critical endemic |
| Population | 90 (in 2004) |
| Where found | Mackenzie Basin |
| Lifespan | 15 years or more |
| Size | 220 g; 40 cm |
| Breeding | September–December; most breed at 3 years of age |
| Nest sites | a scrape in shingle |
| Clutch size | 4 eggs |
| Feeding | insects, fish, molluscs |
| Behaviour | solitary, can be aggressive |

Of the wading birds that inhabit the tussock-covered Mackenzie Basin, the kaki or black stilt has the braided rivers, wetland and lakes largely to itself in winter. Unlike other waders such as the banded dotterel, wrybill or pied stilt, the world's rarest wading bird does not migrate to warmer northern estuaries and mudflats. Instead it revels in the harsh climate of the Mackenzie, where temperatures plummet well below zero on the coldest nights: one tough bird. And yet despite its capacity to cope with such adverse conditions, the black stilt's existence hangs by a fragile thread.

It has been that way since the 1950s. Back then the population was estimated at about 50, a dismal fact known chiefly by worried ornithologists. Even when Ranger Dave Murray, formerly the programme manager for the black stilt rescue effort, joined the Wildlife Service in 1972, the bird did not yet have the dubious distinction of being known as the 'world's rarest wader'. But today its fame is spread far and wide, with any news of the stilt flashed to an attentive international audience.

The numbers game is always a difficult one though. Dave Murray explains that when the stilts were first put under the microscope, several factors combined to make it hard to estimate accurate numbers. 'In the days when we started intensive scrutiny, we had difficulty with precise counting because we didn't have them all banded, we couldn't recognise individuals and we were quoting everything in the population, including juveniles. But now we count only the adults, simply because so many of the young ones don't survive. So what we do is quote the number that survive till adulthood and that gives a reasonable trend from year to year. Also in the early days there might have been confusion with what we call black stilts because of the dark hybrids that were included in the population. Now we talk about pure black stilts,' says Murray.

In the last four years, since DOC started releasing quite a number of captive birds into the breeding population, numbers have been on the rise. By 2001 there were 47 adults in the wild; in 2004 the number had climbed to sixty-eight. Those 68 divided into 30 females and 38 males. Of these adults, there are just 13 breeding pairs. In captivity there were 22 adults (10 females, 12 males, five productive pairs).

It was largely thanks to the work of then Otago University scientist Ray Pierce that the world learned about the plight of the feisty kaki, so named by Maori because of its yapping cry. As a boy, Pierce spent his holidays in the Mackenzie where he first got to know the distinctive black stilt. As a scientist, he began his PhD study into the birds in the late 1970s. He discovered that a multitude of factors had led to its decline. Changes to its habitat, the arrival of predators and hybridisation with the recent Australian migrant the pied stilt had together imperilled the black stilt.

DAVE MURRAY

■ In order to maintain the proper incubation temperature, the kaki mother must turn or rotate her eggs several times a day. She hops on the rim of the nest and gently rolls the eggs with her bill.

Today the black stilt lives in and around braided rivers. Relatively rare habitats in themselves (outside of the South Island's east coast they are found only in the Himalayas, Siberia, Alaska and the Andes), braided rivers wend sinuous trails to the sea, forming many channels between islands of gravel. Here the birds breed between September and January. Once the breeding season is over, the stilts fly to nearby glacial-fed lakes such as Tekapo, Pukaki, Ohau and Benmore, where they find abundant invertebrates and fish on the extensive river deltas. And yet up until the nineteenth century the kaki was widespread throughout New Zealand, breeding from Rotorua down to Otago. Today their range has contracted to the upper Waitaki Basin.

From the 1950s to the 1970s, the character of the Mackenzie Basin changed as massive earth-moving equipment created dams, canals and artificial lakes for hydroelectric schemes. This destroyed some of the stilt's habitat, although today there is still more habitat available than there are black stilts to occupy it. Furthermore, dams have not disfigured rivers like the upper Rangitata, where the species used to live. Other, subtler changes have had adverse effects on the habitat. Introduced plants such as multicoloured flowering broom and lupin have colonised the natural riverbeds. These plants have changed the riverbeds' character, making them less suitable as breeding sites. They also now provide cover for cats and ferrets that stalk unwary nesting stilts.

Ferrets and cats have had a devastating effect on the stilt. Ray Pierce's work showed that only one egg out of 100 laid had any chance of becoming an adult because of predation. And yet the black stilt's relative the pied stilt, which arrived from Australia only several hundred years ago, inhabits the same area and manages to cope with predators. Why the difference?

There are several answers. One is that in its native Australia, the pied stilt has learned to live with predators for thousands of years and has means of evading them, whereas the black stilt is still a novice when dealing with mammal predators, which first reached New Zealand only several hundred years ago. Black stilt pairs are solitary and prefer to nest on dry banks of streams or ponds, which are easy for predators to reach; pied stilts, on the other hand, nest on islands surrounded by water and in the company of other stilts, offering more security.

The black stilt is not as skilled as the pied stilt at distracting predators away from a nest either. If a predator is in the neighbourhood, the adult pied stilt pretends to be injured, drawing the predator away from the nest with a seemingly broken wing. By contrast, the black stilt appears to have lost this protective distracting behaviour. Finally, a black stilt chick takes longer to become a fledgling – 40 days

DOC

Beautiful though they may be, Russell lupins introduced from Europe and North America have altered braided river habitats, crowding out bird nest sites.

As a species black stilts have been separated from pied stilts (pictured) for perhaps a million years, although the two interbreed.

compared to 30 for the pied stilt – so it is vulnerable for a much longer time.

The third key factor that has endangered the black stilt is hybridisation. Although black stilts prefer to breed with their own kind, because there are so few they sometimes opt to breed with pied stilts. This has been the case with male black stilts, which used to outnumber females two to one, although with recent releases the balance between males and females seems to have been restored. The hybrid chicks that result then tend to adopt pied habits, such as migrating to North Island harbours in spring.

Following the completion of his doctorate, Ray Pierce's chief recommendations were to take eggs from nests, incubate them, then return them to black stilt pairs just before they hatched, and to erect electric fences around several nest sites.

'I guess that was the lowest period,' says Dave Murray in retrospect. 'From 1981 to 1983 we counted about 23 adults in the wild. We didn't know the ages of those birds but we probably had an old breeding population. If we hadn't started a rescue

DAVE MURRAY

■ It's a family affair: male and females both help to build the nest, they carry on this cooperative approach through to incubation, taking turns to sit on the nest for about an hour at a time.

■ Brooder aviary at Twizel where black stilt chicks are raised before release into the wild.

programme then we would really have been on the brink. They could have easily gone into extinction at that stage if we hadn't done anything.'

In fact, steps had already been taken in 1979 to boost the population by transferring eight eggs from three nests from the Mackenzie Basin to the Mt Bruce Wildlife Centre in the Wairarapa. From that point on, every egg from every known stilt nest was removed for artificial incubation. In doing so, wildlife managers encourage the stilts to re-nest up to three or four times a season, because the birds replace the eggs that have been removed.

Between 1979 and 1999, 499 eggs were incubated and returned to stilt parents. On the face of it, this number would seem to be a huge boost to the population, but it soon became apparent that the chicks were not surviving. Of all those eggs that hatched, only 17 per cent managed to reach fledgling stage (about 40 days old). The cause of death for 45 per cent of them was predation. And of those that reached fledgling stage, few survived to finally become breeding adults.

Plainly, the strategy of relying on black stilts to raise the chicks was not working. But trying to isolate the reasons why was not easy. Some nests that were protected from predators were more successful than nests not safeguarded, but even so, few birds were graduating to become breeders. Conservation managers pinpointed one reason early on. Sometimes, because there were not sufficient black stilt parents, eggs were placed with black stilt/pied stilt parents. However, the latter parents invariably migrated away in the summer, the young followed them and were then lost to the black stilt breeding population.

It was time for a rethink. In 1988 DOC (itself a fledgling agency having been formed in 1987) carried out an audit of the black stilt programme. 'We were a bit stuck in the late 80s; we were working with pretty limited funds at that stage and the project was looked at by people within and outside DOC,' says Dave Murray. 'They made some recommendations that we were doing the right thing but we needed to do more of it. They said we had to focus more on captive management, so since that time most of our effort has gone there. They also recommended that we do more work on hybridisation, and that we find out more about the cause of nesting failures.'

Captive breeding had begun in 1979 with the hatching of the eight eggs at the Mt Bruce Wildlife Centre, and the birds became the nucleus of a rearing programme. During the early 1980s a number of their offspring were released into the Mackenzie Basin at one year of age, but only one survived past a month. They were too tame, and their time in the secure Mt Bruce facility had not prepared them for dealing with predators. This costly mistake persuaded conservation managers to

DAVE MURRAY

■ Kaki chicks are not as helpless as they might appear. Within a few hours of hatching, they move away from the nest to explore their surroundings, but never stray far.

build an aviary at Twizel in the Mackenzie Basin itself. Advised Ray Pierce: 'No further liberations should take place until the habitat in captive pens can be made to resemble that in the wild more closely.'

A first aviary was built in 1987, followed by a second in 1988 and a third in 1991. If the facility is operating at maximum production (which depends on the eggs available), it can in theory turn out 85 chicks a year, and the Isaac Wildlife Trust at Peacock Springs near Christchurch can rear about another fifteen. Chicks are released at differing times, usually either three or nine months. The three-month-old juveniles are released at that age to make way for more chicks hatched later in the season, as there is simply not enough room in the aviaries for a large number of juveniles during winter.

While three-month-old stilts would appear to be less ready to confront the rigours of life in the Mackenzie Basin than at nine months, recent survival rates have been good. The first year of such early releases was 1999, when nine out of the 10 juveniles survived the winter. 'Ninety per cent survived, showing us that releasing young birds in summer was an option for us. This has enabled us to run the aviary facilities at full capacity, knowing that we do not need to provide facilities for all the juveniles over winter,' says Dave Murray.

Starvation is the second chief reason why juveniles die. Therefore, when released they are given supplementary food for the first month, by which time they have

DAVE MURRAY

■ Birds released into the wild are fed and monitored daily until they disperse from the release site or lose interest in the supplementary food. A lack of iodine initially caused some young birds to die, but this was rectified by adding it to their supplementary diet.

weaned themselves off the handouts and are completely feeding from the wild. Because a number of birds have died from goitre, iodine is now added to their diet.

The problem of hybridisation with pied stilts appears to be on the wane as the population of black stilts increases, says Murray. DNA analysis has confirmed that pure black birds are pure black stilts, with more white feathers the less pure they are. DOC has begun some further DNA work to satisfy themselves as to the purity of the species. Hybridisation has happened because the population is so low, rather than something that caused it to be so low. Since black stilts prefer to mate with a black stilt, care is taken to ensure that there is a potential black mate available when the captive-bred yearlings are released.

Predators will always be a major problem for the black stilt. Dave Murray says DOC is doing what it can to find better ways to control predators: 'If we are ever going to manage kaki in the wild without captive management we have to find a better way to control predators or put more effort into controlling them around nest sites.' Cats, ferrets, rats, black-backed gulls, harriers and hedgehogs are all capable of eating either the birds or eggs. Stilts regularly drive harrier hawks away from nesting areas but they are far less effective at dealing with mammalian predators. A student researcher has tried to train them to react to a cat. Even though there was a measurable response, there was no measurable improvement in the survival of those that had been trained compared to others.

The average age of the black stilts is about six years (of those that survive the first year). Some bred in captivity have lived to about 13, and there is a record of one in the wild surviving until over fifteen. The birds are not mature till two, and generally they do not breed till they are in their third year – so with a bird that on average lives to six, they do not have the luxury of much time on their side to augment the population.

Despite the population increase, the stilts have not expanded their range far beyond the Mackenzie Basin. Wandering birds have turned up throughout Canterbury and on the West Coast but there are no pairs outside the Mackenzie – a situation DOC is happy with as the black stilts are more likely to breed with their own kind if they are not scattered far and wide.

The annual budget of the black stilt programme is $380,000 a year, but to those who work on the project and to many watching and willing the programme on, it is all money well spent.

# Project River Recovery

Crucial to the upturn in fortunes of the black stilt is Project River Recovery, a scheme that began in 1991, and which aims to restore the rivers and wetlands of the upper Waitaki Basin. The programme is funded by Meridian Energy, formerly the Electricity Corporation of New Zealand, to the tune of about $400,000 a year, and is the outcome of a Compensatory Funding Agreement which recognises the impact of hydroelectric schemes on the environment of the area. This money is used for developing or maintaining wetlands, researching predator control and weed control.

Mark Sanders, DOC manager in charge of Project River Recovery, emphasises that the project is designed to protect and enhance the area's habitat for all native plants and animals, and not just for the flagship endangered species such as the black stilt. 'People were very much bird oriented in the first few years but we have decided to try and look after the whole habitat,' he says. Among the special plants and animals of the braided river habitat are:

- More than a dozen species of native birds;
- The endangered robust grasshopper;
- Skinks, geckos, fish and a variety of insects;
- Low-growing perennial native plants.

Some of the original intentions of the project have changed since its creation. Take

# There came a little black bird

New Zealand is well known in sporting circles for its All Blacks. The ornithological world knows it better for another group of 'all blacks': its black-coloured birds which include the Chatham Island black robin, the Snares Island tomtit, the black oystercatcher, the South Island fantail, the black stilt, and a number of shags.

DAVE MURRAY

Termed 'melanism', this tendency towards black shading is regarded in other regions of the world as a sign of adaptive regression. However, the explanation for New Zealand

■ Young black stilts are born with extensive areas of white but between 14 and 20 months they attain the all-black plumage of an adult.

birds is different: because they lived on islands with few predators, they did not have to evolve the elaborate counter-shading that protects birds elsewhere.

Another theory holds that birds switch to black in order to retain heat in a cooler climate. This certainly could be the case for the black stilt, which is closely related to the Australian pied stilt and presumably would once have resembled it. Since its arrival in New Zealand some thousands of years ago, it has given up its black and white markings for its current all-black strip.

wetland construction, for example. Around 100 hectares of wetlands have been artificially created, while existing wetlands and lakes have been enlarged. However, Mark Sanders believes there is a more important priority than building wetlands. 'It's much more cost-effective to protect the ones that we've got. We are still losing wetlands; we don't begin to do enough to protect those that exist,' he says.

Since 1850, 40 per cent of the wetlands in the upper Waitaki have been drained for farming, and only 20 per cent of what remains is of high quality. Sanders explains that between Twizel and Omarama there were once thousands of hectares of wetland sedge plants. Despite that, the new wetlands have proved their worth. Black stilts, black-fronted terns, South Island pied oystercatchers and banded dotterels are just four of the 25 bird species that use them for feeding in and nesting by.

The wetlands have been invaluable for use in research into ways of protecting birds from predators. Chief dangers to wildlife are wild cats, ferrets, hedgehogs (they

DAVE MURRAY

■ Community support is an important aspect of the kaki programme. Mackenzie Basin locals participate in a juvenile release on the Ahuriri River.

■ Tekapo released stilts en masse

■ It might be September, but the Mackenzie Basin still wears the frozen landscape of winter. Nine-month-old juveniles are released into this challenging environment by Girl Guides.

eat eggs), stoats, and birds such as the harrier hawk, black-backed gull and magpie. The latter are less of a problem than the introduced mammals. A more recent twist to the predator question has been the introduction of rabbit haemorrhagic disease (RHD) – formerly known as RCD – in the late 1990s. Before some farmers released it illegally, scientists had warned that cats and ferrets, whose main diet was rabbit, might switch to birds when the rabbits died from the disease. Project River Recovery is attempting to discover whether their worst fears have been founded.

Scientists have also been testing to see whether a combination of electric fencing and trapping can assist birds to breed. The results have been encouraging, showing that egg survival rates are two to three times greater within the fence than outside, and chick survival is better. Other research projects under way in the upper Waitaki are:

- Video filming at nests to see which predators are killing which birds;
- The use of transmitters on black-fronted terns and banded dotterels;
- Studies to find out if the population of the wrybill (a bird with the only sideways curved beak in the world) is increasing, decreasing or remaining stable;
- Investigating how far hedgehogs roam and what their diet consists of;
- Finding the best way of poisoning wild cats.

■ The Godley River, which feeds Lake Tekapo, is a braided river where significant numbers of black stilts have been released in recent years.

The third prong of the programme is weed control. Braided riverbeds have been crowded out by lupins, crack willows, gorse, broom and other introduced plants, smothering nest sites and replacing the shallow edges, where most wading birds feed, with steep-sided river channels. But what to some is a weed, is to many others an attractive wildflower. Russell lupins, which carpet the Mackenzie Basin in gaudy shades of mauve, pink and purple during summer, are a case in point. Along with their cousin, the yellow tree lupin, they colonise riverbeds, demolishing the habitat of native species. In fact, many people believe that the Russell lupin is a native plant.

Since 1991, Project River Recovery has controlled these invasive weeds in more than 33,000 hectares of riverbed. However, as Mark Sanders is quick to point out, that ought not create an image of weed exterminators armed with spraypacks dosing the high country in a haphazard fashion: 'We aren't spraying everywhere. The type of weeds and their density varies from place to place. We have a site-management plan for each area. For example, in the Godley River there's not much sweet briar so it's easy to control there, but in the Tekapo River it's beyond control so we don't even try. We are also trying to take the heat out of the lupin debate as

DAVE MURRAY

■ The existing wetland of Mick's Lagoon in the upper Waitaki has been enlarged and surrounded by a predator exclusion fence.

there are a lot of other plants which are much worse, such as purple loosestrife, which is a major pest in the United States and has the potential of becoming a big weed problem here,' says Sanders. Among the achievements are:

- Bulldozers and diggers removing crack willows from 160 hectares of the Tekapo Delta and from 350 hectares of the lower Ahuriri River;
- Lupins, gorse, broom and willow controlled on 3000 hectares of the Tekapo River and on 350 hectares of the lower Ahuriri River;
- Other weeds reined in, in over more than 25,000 hectares of the Tasman, Cass, Godley, Hopkins, Dobson and Macaulay rivers.

Depending on the need, Project River Recovery may continue through to the time when Meridian's water rights expire in 2024. Every seven years the funding and direction of the programme is reviewed; the end of the second seven-year period is in 2005.

## References

Maloney, Richard, and Murray, David, *Kaki (black stilt) recovery plan 2001–2011*, Department of Conservation, 2001.

# 4 Chatham Island Oystercatcher

*Robust wader of the rocky coast*

| | |
|---|---|
| Scientific name | *Haematopus chathamensis* |
| Popular name | Chatham Island oystercatcher |
| Conservation status | protected nationally critical endemic |
| Population | 220 + (in 2004) |
| Where found | main Chatham Island, South East (Rangatira) Island, Pitt Island |
| Life span | 7.7 years |
| Size | 600 g; 48 cm |
| Breeding | October–February; can start breeding at 3 years of age, most begin at 5–6 |
| Nest sites | a scrape in the sand or among rocks |
| Clutch size | 2 eggs |
| Feeding | oysters, mussels, limpets, marine worms, small invertebrates |
| Behaviour | attacks predators in groups; pretends to be injured to lure intruders away from nest |

PETER MOORE

rances Schmechel is no casual birdwatcher. Between 1994 and 1997 the United States-born naturalist spent six months each year on the Chatham Islands, her binoculars trained on one of the rarest and most endangered birds in the world.

Never common at the best of times, the Chatham Island oystercatcher's fortunes appeared to take a turn for the worse in the 1970s and 1980s as its population plummeted to around 50 birds – although there is debate about the figure because of flawed censuses. Some estimate it may have been as high as one hundred. Studying for her PhD, Frances' task was fourfold: to count the population; analyse the major threats to the bird's survival; assess their habitat requirements; and study their behaviour.

It was not always an easy doctoral assignment. Lying on sharp marram grass spikes under a hot sun, collecting prickly bidibid seeds in her clothes, warding off territorial birds and living the self-imposed lifestyle of a hermit, she sometimes questioned the wisdom of what she had taken on. However, the combination of persistence and determination has paid off, seeing that in the years since she left the island, the oystercatcher's numbers have doubled to more than two hundred and twenty.

It was not what she imagined she might end up doing when she arrived in New Zealand on a Rotary Scholarship in the early 1990s. At the time she was with the US

PETER MOORE

■ Oystercatcher habitat and encroaching marram vegetation on dunes of the Maunganui coast, northern Chatham Island.

FRANCES SCHMECHEL

■ Frances Schmechel at work measuring eggs at an oystercatcher nest.

FRANCES SCHMECHEL

Forest Service, carrying out habitat assessments. At Lincoln University she enrolled in the School of Resource Management, chiefly a breeding ground for policy makers and planners. But a desk-bound career did not appeal to Frances, who, having completed a diploma now sought a position with the Department of Conservation. That was in April 1994. By October she was on the Chathams, focusing her binoculars on what she came to regard as 'fascinating birds'. Frances is modest about her role in this recovery story. She regards her research as the catalyst which resulted in a number of measures being taken to safeguard the oystercatcher, most important among these being to protect the coastal species from predators.

■ LEFT: Chatham Island Oystercatchers size up a 'model' intruder.
BELOW: A double-sized model attracts a lot of attention. Even though it is somewhat intimidating, it can still not be tolerated and is dealt to.

FRANCES SCHMECHEL

Marauding cats are the oystercatcher's chief enemy on main Chatham Island where the bulk of the population occurs. According to DOC scientist Peter Moore, 'I don't think I've been in a place where I've seen so many cats. You see them when you're driving along the road in scrubby areas; there must be thousands if not hundreds of thousands on the island.' Nature also plays a part in keeping the population low. Some years when the stocky oystercatcher nests along the coastline, its fragile scrape in the sand is overwhelmed by storms and its precious eggs are swept away on a turbulent tide.

When Frances began her study, little was known about the birds and their requirements, even their numbers. It was known that the Chatham Island species was smaller and stockier than its mainland cousins, and that it had larger feet. This latter point is significant, since the bird spends more time on and around rocks than other oystercatchers, hence the need for larger feet to grip on tight.

Since humans arrived on the Chathams, a number of changes have impacted upon the oystercatcher. The first settlers, Moriori, brought with them the kiore or Polynesian rat, which would have eaten eggs but probably not the actual bird. Fortunately the kuri or Maori dog, which would have created havoc among many of the indigenous species, never accompanied the Moriori.

Even though the main Chatham Island is a reasonable size at 100,000 hectares, the percentage that is usable habitat is quite small, since the bird lives along the coast and often prefers rocky areas to sandy. Their most favoured haunts tend to be on the northern coast in the core territories of Maunganui and Wharekauri.

These were the questions Frances wanted answered:

- What is the population size, is it growing or diminishing, and what is the male to female ratio or the adult to juvenile ration?
- What are the factors limiting and regulating the population?
- Has the introduction of marram grass significantly changed sand-dune structures and therefore decreased the availability of nesting habitats?
- What is the productivity of the birds and what percentage are attempting to breed?
- Is estimated productivity sufficient to maintain or increase the population over the long term?
- When are the eggs and chicks dying and what are the causes?
- Do territorial birds remain in territories during the winter or do they flock together? If they form flocks, at what point do they leave to defend a territory?
- Where do young birds disperse?
- Do young birds mix with other birds during the winter or are they excluded from certain favoured areas?
- What should the recovery goals be?

PETER MOORE

■ Stacy Moore and an oystercatcher chick ready for banding.

Before 1998 there had not been a systematic, comprehensive survey of the population. It was difficult for the few people working on the oystercatcher to cover the whole coastline, so qualifications had to be applied to any census. In 1986–87 the estimated total was 55–65; 1987–88, 103–110; 1993–94, 69–73; and by 1996 it had risen to between 100 and one hundred and twenty. Despite the increase between 1993 and 1996, Frances herself observed no breeding. By the time of the first proper census in 1998, there were 142 oystercatchers.

Fortunately the oystercatcher is a long-lived bird, so that those lucky enough to survive past a critical period could be expected to live on for 25 to 30 years. Even though birds were failing to breed much, most of those that did reach adulthood faced a small risk of dying. Overall annual mortality is a low six per cent.

However, a lack of knowledge about the historical level of the oystercatcher population makes it difficult to set a target for what would be an ideal population size, says Frances. There are two possibilities regarding past population levels: one, that the population was always low, and intervention may not be required; or more likely, she believes, that numbers have dropped following human arrival.

On a typical day Frances would observe the birds, check on pairs breeding and note their behaviour and habitat. She mapped the entire habitat around the island

and measured whether the birds were using all of it. Using a farm bike, walking or boating to 'work', she generally found her day exhilarating and enjoyable, although much depended on the fickle Chathams weather: 'I spent a lot of time sneaking up on birds, laying in the dunes, and every five minutes I'd record all their behaviours. It's a windy place; everything I did the wind got in the way, and one day I just had to let out a big scream at one point. It was uncomfortable among the marram grass and the bidibids attached themselves to everything, but there were no sandflies, which was very convenient.'

By the third year of the study, Frances found that she was making progress and that she was more focused in her research. The best part was watching the birds and recording their daily rituals. 'I love the oystercatchers. They are fantastic birds, real comical characters. I created cardboard models of other oystercatchers and observed how territorial they are. They would just go berserk and attack the models.'

The end of Frances' work with the oystercatchers coincided with a change of conservation management in the Chathams, and consequently a boost in funding for all critically endangered species there. The Wellington conservancy of DOC took over the running of the Chathams programmes from Canterbury.

Frances rates her work as having raised the profile of the oystercatcher's plight, especially in the Chathams community. She printed a newsletter for households, visited the local school and generally communicated what she had found. But most importantly, she had identified the barriers that were standing in the way of the oystercatcher developing a self-sustaining population. Now her recommendations could be put into effect.

Peter Moore, whose main focus for much of his scientific life had been the yellow-eyed penguin, takes up the story. 'We decided to concentrate on those areas where most oystercatchers are found, which is in the north of the main island. There were two major priorities: one to catch predators; the other to assist the birds whose nests were being swamped by the tide,' he says.

# Trapping programme

Cats were, and are, the greatest threat. During summer a trapping programme kills the resident cats and keeps the immigrant cats down to a low level in order to allow the eggs and chicks to survive. 'It's a thin line on the coast about 14 kilometres long, and we've got these small trapping operations in these very small areas. We have been catching up to 50 cats a year in some areas, and in others up to 100 a year. All the time there are cats trickling in. We just keep the numbers down in a small area and that seems to be the key to our success.'

PETER MOORE

■ A cat caught in a trap casts a baleful eye at its captor. The controlling of cats in key areas has been a major reason for an increase in oystercatcher numbers.

PETER MOORE

■ Weka, introduced to the Chathams in 1905, are opportunistic predators.

Peter is resigned to the fact that cats will always be a part of the environment on the island, unpalatable though it might be to accept. And even in the unlikely event that all Chatham Islanders decided against having moggies, the chances of ridding the island of feral cats are slim. After all, it took several years of immense effort to kill the last cats on 2817-hectare Little Barrier Island, miniscule in size beside 100,000-hectare Chatham Island. The best that might be hoped for is that the islanders neuter their cats. Smaller Pitt Island has a resident population of oystercatchers and just a few farming families. With their co-operation cats could be exterminated, he believes. The Department of Conservation is not pressing the issue, but is hopeful that the growing conservation awareness that has taken root will bring about change.

Conservation managers were able to monitor nests by setting up video cameras.

# Family ties

**The Chatham Island oystercatcher is just one of three oystercatcher species found in New Zealand. On the mainland, the high-pitched, shrill 'kleep' calls of the pied oystercatcher (*Haematopus ostralegus*) and the variable oystercatcher (*Haematopus unicolor*) are common during the breeding season.**

Virtually worldwide in its distribution, the pied oystercatcher (also known as the South Island pied oystercatcher or SIPO) has a population of more than 85,000 in New Zealand. Early European settlers hunted it, killing large numbers, but since the 1940s it has thrived, part of the reason being an increase in pastoral lands in the South Island where it breeds. Oddly enough, the pied oystercatcher breeds only alongside riverbeds; their young do not get a whiff of salt water until they migrate in late summer to northern wintering-over areas such as the Kaipara and Manukau harbours, or the Firth of Thames.

The variable oystercatcher is a rarer bird with a population of around four thousand. It is found only in New Zealand, living along the coast, and often remains in the same location year-round. As its name implies, the variable oystercatcher changes colour with latitude: the further south, the greater the number of the species sporting a jet-black coloration. In northern New Zealand about 43 per cent are pure black, in the middle of the country the percentage rises to 85, and in the south of the South Island 94 per cent are black.

All oystercatchers throughout the world share similarly coloured red legs, to match their red bill and red circles around their eyes. The *Haematopus* name given to the genus, meaning 'blood legs', acknowledges this striking characteristic.

The question of when the oystercatcher arrived in the Chathams, and to which species on the mainland it is related, have not been answered. Peter Moore, who specialises in the conservation

Over three summers these captured 19 nest failures, 13 of them because of cats. Some, but not all, cats have learned the trick of breaking eggs and eating the contents. 'Cats take eggs from the nest, but the adult bird flies away just in time. A lot of people might not realise that's how it happens because you think of cats eating chicks and adults. They found that on the braided river studies in the Tekapo area. It seems to be a learned behaviour because we've seen a number of cats which haven't been able to break into the eggs. But once they've learned it they'll come back again and again. In our unmanaged areas the birds would lose their eggs every time to the same-looking cat. There was obviously a resident cat which would just find the nests when it wanted to have a meal and that would be the end of any nesting attempt,' says Peter.

Weka were also caught stabbing at eggs and eating them. Between 500 and 700

and ecology of seabirds and shorebirds, says that as yet no DNA study has been carried out on the New Zealand oystercatchers. Oystercatchers throughout the world are so similar in look and behaviour that it is evident they have only recently spread out from wherever they originated.

While the Chatham Island species is a pied variety, and therefore might be thought to be closer to the South Island pied, it is coastal, highly territorial and lives all year round in the same seashore habitat – all characteristics typical of the variable oystercatcher.

The oystercatcher's fierce defence of its nest and territory is a defining attribute. On the Chathams the birds defend their territories throughout the year, but become especially uncompromising with intruders during breeding. In the densest, most sought-after areas, each territory may be only 100 metres long. Peter Moore says some birds would come from one kilometre away to investigate an approaching person.

Like others who have closely observed the birds, Peter admires them for their pluckiness and survival skills. 'I think they are very character-filled, alert birds, that defend their patch fiercely. They have a high-pitched call, which is especially strident when they are on the boundary of their territory – then they run around like a little motorised bird chasing threats away. They have different behaviours depending on the stage of the breeding cycle. At the egg stage they are very furtive; if there's any disturbance they quickly depart the nest and lurk in the background trying to keep a low profile and if necessary they will leave the area. More frequently you will see them trying to hide, sticking their head behind a clump of flax away from the nest. Once the chicks are hatched the parents will chase whoever is in the area, and swoop at them,' he says. They are animals well adapted to conditions on the Chatham Islands before humans arrived, he adds.

weka a year were trapped near the oystercatchers' main breeding grounds. It is ironic that the buff weka thrives on Chatham Island, to which it was introduced in the nineteenth century from the South Island's east coast, where it is now extinct.

# Habitat improvements

The second main prong of the DOC approach is to improve the birds' habitat.

'Introduced marram grass has been very successful at binding sand but the profile of the beaches has changed. Before that, pingao was the main sedge plant, along with small herbaceous plants including the Chatham Island forget-me-not which is very palatable to sheep. Our theory is that so many nests get washed away because the birds are forced to nest closer to the high-tide mark by these steeper-faced dunes that have been stabilised by the marram. Before we would have had

A successful trial! A year after marram was cleared and this pingao was planted an oystercatcher nested beside it. The native pingao is a less vigorous sand-binding plant than introduced marram, creating a more open environment suitable for nesting.

PETER MOORE

Alison Davis, DOC area manager for the Chathams, planting akeake to stabilise the back of the dune, shade out the marram, and recreate the succession from seashore to forest to provide a protective habitat for the oystercatchers.

PETER MOORE

The Wharekauri coast, Chatham Island.

PETER MOORE

■ LEFT: The Chatham Island forget-me-not, highly valued by gardeners on the mainland because of its large glossy leaves and attractive blue flowers. It once grew freely along Chathams coasts but now survives only where farm animals cannot reach it. This luxuriant two-year-old plant was planted in an area that was cleared of marram.

■ RIGHT: Frances Schmechel with a newly fledged Chatham Island oystercatcher.

FRANCES SCHMECHEL

REX WILLIAMS

■ One strategy for protecting oystercatcher nests is to place the eggs inside a tyre on a plywood platform, and then shift the nest by degrees up the beach, thus moving it out of the range of storms and high tides.

gentler dunes. So we've started a couple of trials where we've removed the marram and replaced it with pingao, and that's working well so far. For the first time recently one of the oystercatchers has nested right in the pingao,' says Peter.

But until the birds can be persuaded to nest higher up the beach, wildlife managers are giving nature a nudge. If they judge the scrape in the sand to be in danger of being washed away, they surreptitiously shift the nest by degrees further up the beach away from the high-tide mark. 'You move the scrape with a decoration of kelp. You take that decoration a metre away, dig a little scrape and move the eggs away into a new scrape that you've dug, and then destroy the old scrape. Once you move away the bird comes back, and you do the same thing the next day,' says Peter.

A novel method of keeping the nesting oystercatchers out of harm's way is to place car tyres on the beach. The inside is filled with plywood and sand is heaped on top. The fact that the tyre is slightly raised encourages some oystercatchers to nest inside the tyre, which is then shifted incrementally up the beach.

## Declining? Holding its own?

Peter says there has been a quick response to the four-year trapping programme. The first year of trapping produced 17 chicks, the second 25 chicks, the third year nineteen. Oystercatchers can start breeding at two years of age, so already the chicks from the first year are breeding. Peter describes the system as 'dynamic', with birds from non-managed areas coming into the main territories. At the same time there has been a high survival rate; for example, by 2003 there were still 15 of the first cohort of 17 still alive.

So far inbreeding does not seem to be a problem, although Peter notes that there is not enough data to be sure. The signs are good: the birds are fertile, producing up to three chicks a season and there are few deformities. The fact that birds migrate into the managed areas ensures a good gene flow.

Now that the oystercatcher population is a healthy 220 plus, DOC staff will apply what is termed 'pulse management' – in other words they will carry out intensive trapping some years, then less in others. The goal is to produce a self-sustaining population with as little human intervention as possible.

Once Frances Schmechel believed the population might climb to between 250 and 500, but now she imagines that greater than 500 is an attainable figure. There is no shortage of the food that oystercatchers like – molluscs, marine worms and invertebrates – and as numbers increase more and more birds will be forced to nest in less favourable areas.

# 5 Kakapo

## *The boom years are back*

| | |
|---|---|
| Scientific name | *Strigops habroptilus* |
| Popular name | kakapo |
| Conservation status | protected nationally critical endemic |
| Population | 86 (in 2004) |
| Where found | Codfish, Te Kakahu (Fiordland) and Pearl islands |
| Life span | at least 60 years |
| Size | 1.7–4 kg (males), 1.1–2kg (females); 63 cm |
| Breeding | December–March; the kakapo is the only parrot, the only flightless bird, and the only New Zealand bird which is a lek breeder. Under this unusual mating system, the males congregate in an arena to entice females to breed. In order to attract the females they 'boom' by inflating air sacs in their breasts |
| Nest sites | old hollow logs, under tussock |
| Clutch size | 2–4 eggs; two clutches per season possible if first clutch is lost |
| Feeding | fruit, seeds, leaves, stems, and roots |
| Behaviour | nocturnal, flightless and solitary |

DON MERTON

By the early 1980s the bid to boost the numbers of kakapo was stalled. This is not to say that, with many of the known population of around 65 on safe island havens, the world's largest parrot was in danger of extinction. No, it was more that the key to successful breeding of the kakapo was eluding researchers.

But then came a turning point. During the mid to late 1980s, Don Merton, the man behind the black robin rescue and revival, was invited to the island of Mauritius during leave each year to help save the echo parakeet, whose population had tumbled to around eight. Like the kakapo, the parakeet was besieged by introduced mammal predators, and in addition its natural food sources were in a state of near collapse. It soon became apparent that there were many parallels both in the problems confronting the two native island species – and in the solutions.

With little time to lose, Merton, with his many New Zealand and Mauritian co-workers and successors, applied to the parakeet some of the lessons learned from endangered New Zealand species: they protected nests and built nest boxes; they restored habitat; controlled pests such as rats; supplied extra food and manipulated breeding by removing eggs so the birds would lay more eggs. The result is that by 2003 the population of the parakeet had recovered to around 150 and New

## KEY KAKAPO DATES

**circa 1300**   Maori term the parrot 'kaka-po' (kaka of the night)

**1845**   First scientifically described by George Gray as *Strigops* (owl-face) *habroptilus* (soft-feathered)

**1908**   Richard Henry resigns as curator of Resolution Island after 14 years of moving almost 400 kakapo to islands in Dusky Sound, Fiordland

**1927**   Last record of a kakapo in the North Island (Urewaras)

**1958**   Kakapo found in the Tutoko Valley, Fiordland

**1974**   The first of 18 kakapo discovered in Fiordland and the current rescue–recovery thrust involving transfer to, and management on, islands commenced

**1977**   A population estimated at between 100 and 200 is found in a remote corner of Stewart Island

**1980**   First female found since early 1900s on Stewart Island, so ending a 20-year quest to locate females

**1981**   First (two) nests found in living memory on Stewart Island – the first recorded breeding

Zealand's reputation for can-do conservation had yet again been borne out.

One of the key factors in bringing the parakeet back from the brink had been the use of supplementary food to stimulate and support breeding. Studies with kakapo on Stewart Island during the 1980s were pointing to food as being a possible trigger for kakapo breeding. In the light of the parakeet experience, was the answer supplementary feeding or was there a need for an abundant supply of natural foods?

Merton and kakapo scientists Hugh Best, Brian Lloyd and Ralph Powlesland were not the first to speculate about the importance of food to kakapo breeding. Richard Henry, who worked as curator of Resolution Island in Fiordland between 1894 and 1908, tried to usher as many kakapo as possible into safety there and on other nearby islands and was the most astute of the early observers. He noted that the kakapo did not breed every season and wondered whether it related to their supply of food during the previous winter. After puzzling over the question for years, he finally admitted he was at a loss to explain their erratic breeding behaviour.

Almost a century later, pieces of the reproductive jigsaw puzzle started to fall into place. In 1981, kakapo breeding was recorded on Stewart Island, and it occurred

| | |
|---|---|
| **1982** | The first 21 of the Stewart Island kakapo are transferred to Little Barrier Island |
| **1987** | Last record of kakapo in Fiordland |
| **1989** | Supplementary feeding of kakapo on Little Barrier Island is trialled – two nests found in early 1990 |
| **1989** | Comalco begins kakapo sponsorship |
| **1991** | Two male kakapo hatched and raised on Little Barrier Island |
| **1992** | Disastrous first breeding season on Codfish Island – natural food crop fails and chicks starve; Hoki, the first kakapo to be hand-raised, is the sole survivor |
| **1993** | Supplementary feeding begun for Codfish Island kakapo |
| **1997** | The last Stewart Island kakapo – a female – discovered and shifted to Codfish Island |
| **1999** | The last of the kakapo removed from Little Barrier Island |
| **2002** | Twenty-four kakapo hatched, bringing total to eighty-six |
| **2003** | Last five kakapo removed from Maud Island |

again in 1985. Both years were rimu 'masting' seasons, a time when the podocarp produces a superabundance of fruit. Masting is not a phenomenon confined to rimu: many plant species are 'boom and bust' fruiters, responding to climatic variation or simply in order to recover from the effort of a big fruiting season.

In the days when kakapo were widespread throughout New Zealand, it need not have been rimu that sparked breeding. Other plants are more dominant in other areas and their flowers and fruits would have been vital for breeding; for example, when male kakapo boomed (in preparation to breed) in Fiordland during the 1970s and 1980s, it was associated with heavy snow tussock seeding. On Stewart and Codfish islands, rimu is the major forest tree, hence the birds' reliance on it; beech trees are the principal fruiting trees on Te Kakahu (Chalky) Island where 19 kakapo now live.

But just why do kakapo need the security of a good food supply to breed? The female lays two to three, occasionally four eggs, each the size only of a bantam hen's, but she may have to double her energy intake to produce these eggs. Then, once she has hatched the chicks, she has to feed them for more than five months by herself, by which time they could be a hefty 1.5–2 kilograms. Her nightly forays to look for food can mean she must walk several kilometres two or three times a night. Males use up significant amounts of energy when booming. They bulk up by as much as 100 per cent or more of their normal weight in order to come into breeding condition, and have been known to boom each night for three months without a let-up. On one night a male may boom as much as 17,000 times; the deep resonant sound carrying as far as five kilometres.

The kakapo's yo-yo diet would put the most excessive Hollywood star's weight gain and loss regime to shame. Merton contends that its weight changes are the most extreme of any land bird. With its ultra-low metabolism, the kakapo gets by most of the time on a poor diet of leaves, stems and roots, but it is not sufficient to support a family. When eating fibrous foods they extract the nutrients, leaving behind the remains which are an obvious clue that kakapo are in the vicinity.

In 1989, Little Barrier Island in the Hauraki Gulf was chosen for the first supplementary feeding experiment. Apples, kumara, walnuts and almonds made up the extra diet. The result: two females bred for the first time since they were shifted there in 1982, and two males were raised in 1991. Now that the experiment had proved a success, supplementary feeding was extended to kakapo on all islands where they were living, especially on Codfish Island where chicks starved in 1992 because the rimu fruit crop failed.

A glance at the breeding performance of the kakapo over the past 25 years

The kakapo's elaborate mating display at one of its track and bowl systems in Sinbad Valley, Fiordland. This confirmed for Don Merton that the parrot was a lek breeder.

DON MERTON

With no females in Fiordland left to mate with, this kakapo male shifted its attentions to the next closest object – a wildlife officer.

# Comalco and the Kakapo

In the 1970s, New Zealand conservationists, the government and industry were locked in bitter confrontation over a proposal to raise scenic Lake Manapouri in the South Island, frequently touted as the country's most picturesque lake. The plan was to lift the lake level by 8.4 metres in order to provide more water to turn the giant Manapouri hydro station's turbines, which would in turn power Comalco's proposed Bluff aluminium smelter.

New Zealand had never witnessed a conservation campaign like it. The National Government lost the 1972 election partially as a result of its support for drowning the lake, and the birth of the modern-day conservation movement dates from those tumultuous times. As a result, the lake was not sacrificed for the power scheme and it continues to enchant tourists to this day.

Comalco New Zealand, the smelter company embroiled in the argument, was long tainted by its association with the controversy. But that wasn't all. Critics also alleged that the price Comalco paid for the Manapouri electricity was too low. A new power agreement signed in 1993 supposedly meant a significant increase in the electricity price, but as ever the figure remains confidential. Today, however, relations between the conservation community and Comalco are on an improved footing. The turning point occurred in 1989, when, in one of the largest commitments of its kind ever made, the company decided to sponsor the rescue programme for the kakapo. So successful has the programme been that Comalco is signed as a sponsor until 2008.

From the outset, the sponsorship had the blessing of then Comalco New Zealand managing director, Kerry McDonald, who handed the reins over to Philip Strachan in 2003. McDonald took a strong personal interest in the fate of the kakapo. One of the reasons behind choosing the kakapo was the fact that its stronghold is an island in the deep south, close to the smelter.

Critics have accused Comalco of attempting to conduct a superficial PR exercise to give the company a green gloss and to provide some leverage in negotiations over the possible sale of the Manapouri power station. Is the sponsorship not a cynical way of furthering the company's interests? Early on, McDonald was quick to quash the accusations. 'Any of the issues we have to deal with, such as negotiations on Manapouri and expansion of the smelter, they all stand alone. If we are going to have a substantial presence in New Zealand, if we are going to operate as a New Zealand company, then I regard this as an important adjunct of our position,' he counters.

'Substantial presence' the company does possess. It employs 1400 people, and for the most part owns New Zealand's largest single export-earning plant. A NZ$400 million upgrade in 1995 saw aluminium production increase by 30,000 tonnes per year — from the then current level of 260,000 tonnes per year.

Kerry McDonald, former CEO of Comalco New Zealand, on hand to relocate a kakapo.

One of the spin-offs that McDonald saw occurring was a closer relationship with Comalco's old adversaries, the greens. 'Some of the problems we have had in the past we found have been caused by poor communication, a lack of knowledge on both sides,' he said when announcing the sponsorship.

Since then, as part of the Threatened Species Trust which oversees the programme, Comalco has been sitting in on meetings with DOC and New Zealand's leading conservation group, the Royal Forest and Bird Protection Society.

The sponsor cannot direct DOC as to how a recovery programme should be managed, although it can play a fairly active role. For example, in 1994 Comalco supported a review of the kakapo programme, which involved two international bird experts spending three weeks in New Zealand, travelling the country as part of a three-man team. McDonald is quite upfront about Comalco's role. 'We strongly supported the review, not because DOC wasn't performing but because it is a normal management process. We were four years down the road and it's a good idea to step back and get some expert input,' McDonald he says.

Asked if he felt the sponsorship of the kakapo was worthwhile, McDonald was enthusiastic. 'Apart from building the profile of the kakapo project, the partnership has proved a valuable opportunity to exchange views on wider issues and different viewpoints,' he maintains.

If imitation is the sincerest form of flattery, then Comalco has its fair share of admirers. Other corporates such as the Bank of New Zealand have since become major sponsors of threatened species – the kiwi. As a result of Comalco's lead, species sponsorships are here to stay.

Rugged kakapo habitat, looking down from the Tin Range to Port Pegasus in southern Stewart Island.

Gruesome remains of cat predation on Stewart Island, early 1980s. As the death toll mounted, it became an urgent priority to relocate as many kakapo as could be captured to safe islands.

provides striking evidence of the success of the intensive management programme. From 1977 to 1989, there were just two known breeding years. Since 1990 there have been nine breeding years out of a possible thirteen.

A major review of the programme in 1995 saw a beefing up of measures to ensure the species' survival. Even though the survival rate was a high 98 per cent since all birds had been removed to islands, the total population had fallen to an all-time low of 51 by that year. At that time only one person – Don Merton – worked at the national level full-time on kakapo recovery. By 2003 that number had been boosted to twelve.

# Unrealistic dream

Harking back to his earliest recollections of the kakapo, Don Merton says he was just a 'little kid, growing up in a remote town [Gisborne]' when he first read about the bird. Expeditions had been sent into Fiordland during the early 1950s, and in 1956 Gordon Williams of the Wildlife Service wrote a major paper in the bird magazine *Notornis* summing up all that was known about the kakapo, including reports of recent sightings.

Two years later a kakapo was caught in the Tutoko Valley, Fiordland, followed by several others in the years to come. Soon after that, the boy – Don Merton – whose 'unrealistic dream' had been to work with endangered birds joined Brian Bell in the Fauna Protection Section of the Wildlife Service. Just two people were now responsible for all of New Zealand's endangered species.

Although a few birds had been taken for possible captive breeding in the early 60s, they all died (and were all males anyway so breeding was a forlorn hope). Survival of the species itself also appeared bleak until, in 1974, Merton was given responsibility for the field programme and he and colleagues devised a new management strategy to save the kakapo. This time a modern contrivance – the helicopter – was pressed into service to help an ancient species. It made all the difference, since wildlife teams could be ferried to inaccessible mountainsides in minutes, without the arduous job of hauling heavy packs for days through dripping rainforest.

From 1974 until the end of the 1970s, the Wildlife Service found 18 kakapo in Fiordland. Unfortunately, all were male. Some were relocated onto islands, but of the 18 only 'Richard Henry', the sole bird carrying potentially invaluable Fiordland genes, survives to this day.

Staff working on the programme in those days regret that more effort was not made to rescue more Fiordland kakapo. In the days before DOC, when responsibility for administering natural areas was divided between the Lands and Survey Department and the Forest Service, the Wildlife Service sometimes lacked the clout to influence decisions.

Former Wildlife ranger Richard Anderson blames the Fiordland National Park Board, which administered Fiordland National Park, for its intransigence. 'They said the Fiordland kakapo belonged in Fiordland. To me, it's a tragedy that we lost virtually all of that gene pool,' laments Anderson.

Meanwhile, the discovery of the kakapo on southern Stewart Island in 1977 brought the species a reprieve. 'We found somewhere between 150 and 200 birds. We thought they were safe but then we found cats killing them. There had probably been a low level of cat predation for many years, but perhaps one cat developed a taste for them,' recalls Merton.

Researchers Hugh Best and Rodney Russ argued that dogs should immediately be used to catch females, and Merton added his voice to the chorus of concern. Again, Lands and Survey blocked the way. Their reasons may have been based on a degree of logic – a dog had recently mistakenly killed a kakapo on Maud Island – but as a result they refused to let dogs find kakapo on Stewart Island for three years. During that time, a cat or cats made critical inroads into the population.

Between 1979 and 1992, 85 kakapo were found alive on Stewart Island. But of those, only 61 survived long enough to be transferred to safety on Little Barrier and Codfish islands.

## Safe islands?

But were these islands so safe? Certainly there were no cats, stoats, European rats or possums, but there were kiore which competed with kakapo for food and ate chicks. For years researchers had differing opinions about the impact of kiore. Some believed that while kiore might eat eggs and chicks, their effect was minimal, while others pointed out that with a species as rare as the kakapo, the rat was a significant threat. And it was not just a question of eating eggs and chicks: when kiore scavenged around nests they disturbed young chicks, putting them under stress and sometimes forcing them to expel their precious food.

From 1995 the kakapo became the subject of the most intensive campaign ever to save a bird species. Kiore were now not to be tolerated near nests and a 24-hour guard was kept over nesting birds. Whenever something that was not a kakapo entered a nest an alarm sounded and a watcher set off a 'rat banger', a small explosive charge that scared the interloper away. By 1999, when all the kakapo had been relocated to just two islands, Codfish and Maud, the rats were eradicated from Codfish; none had ever appeared on Maud.

This period marked the time when the movements of every kakapo started to be scrutinised like never before. For some years they had been each fitted with a

DON MERTON

■ Rat traps guard the entrance to a kakapo nest on Codfish Island, 1997. An infra-red beam alerts watchers to the comings and goings of the kakapo mother.

DON MERTON

■ A DOC nest minder settles in for the night with all the essentials needed to pass the time away.

transmitter so that they could always be located. About once a year each bird is caught, given a health check and, if necessary, treated and its transmitter changed.

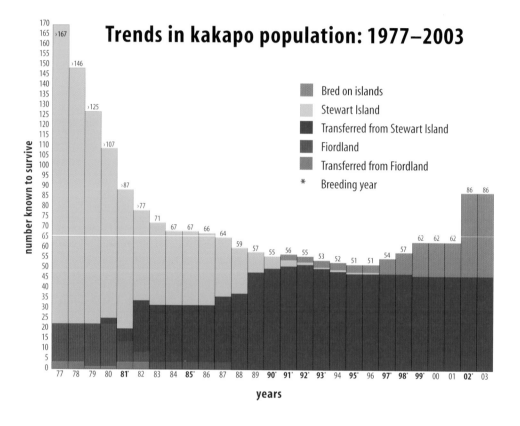

# Trends in kakapo population: 1977–2003

**Legend:**
- Bred on islands
- Stewart Island
- Transferred from Stewart Island
- Fiordland
- Transferred from Fiordland
- \* Breeding year

This policy of close surveillance paid off in 1997 when six kakapo nests were located on Codfish Island. Instantly a 24-hour guard was set up around each nest. Once again the rimu fruit did not ripen, but the supplementary feeding regime proved its value by providing vital support for the breeding females. One chick that was not thriving was removed from the nest and hand-reared. Consequently, three male chicks were added to the population that year, and the kakapo team was also handed a pleasant surprise in the form of the discovery of a female kakapo on Stewart Island – five years after the sixtieth bird had been removed from the island.

The next additions to the kakapo population came from an unexpected quarter. In 1998, a female, which had lived on Little Barrier for 14 years without breeding, was shifted to Maud Island where she nested in a pine plantation. Her mate was Richard Henry, ensuring that some Fiordland kakapo genes would be carried on in the resulting three chicks, one of which was a female.

DON MERTON

Mother and nestling, Codfish Island, 1997. The mother never defecates in the nest, but nestlings do. By the time the juvenile is ready to strike out on its own, its droppings form much of the nest material.

DON MERTON

Zephyr and chick, 1997.

# Essence of kakapo

Kakapo not only possess a keen sense of smell; they also give off a strong scent. Maori hunters knew the truth of the former because they had to approach the birds from downwind when trying to catch them, and Don Merton has stories of kakapo which have dug up foods he had hidden.

The fact that kakapo give off a distinctive odour has been remarked upon by virtually everyone who has ever had some contact with them. They have distinctively sweet feathers which people can detect from several metres away, while dogs with their keen sense of smell can identify them from close to half a kilometre off – or so early conservationist Richard Henry maintained when he observed his own dog reacting to the scent. It is little wonder that the kakapo was such easy prey for Maori dogs, kuri, and later, cats, dogs, stoats and Eurasian rats.

Only recently has this aspect of the kakapo's biology been closely scrutinised. Julie Hagelin, currently a professor at Swarthmore College in the US, has not only discovered fresh insights into

DON MERTON

■ Richard Henry, the only remaining Fiordland kakapo, on Maud Island in 1979, held by Don Merton's son David. Richard Henry is still alive, 30 years after being found in Fiordland, and has managed to pass on his vital genes to the kakapo population.

the kakapo, but her research has also drawn intriguing conclusions about the role of scent in island species. Her investigation looked at the feeding behaviour of the kakapo when offered food from bins. She also had the rare chance of studying a kakapo brain to try and unlock the secret of its advanced sense of smell.

In the feeding experiment on Maud Island in the Marlborough Sounds, Julie presented the celebrated Richard Henry (the only surviving Fiordland/mainland kakapo) with the choice of three food bins at his feeding station. Usually birds receiving supplementary food – consisting at that time of walnuts, brazil nuts, pumpkin seeds, sunflower seeds, kumara and apple – are offered just one bin. Only one of the trial bins contained food. Each day, after the kakapo had visited, the bins were shuffled so that the food was never in the same place that night.

On nine of the 11 nights that Julie carried out the experiment, Richard Henry first opened the bin where food had been the night before. When he discovered it empty, he moved on to the bin where the food actually was. Julie concludes that the experiment showed the kakapo used both memory and smell when foraging. Only one other parrot species has so far shown an ability to discriminate between odours while foraging.

To discover what physically sets the kakapo 'nose' apart from other birds, Julie compared the 'olfactory bulb ratio' (OBR) of the kakapo to other bird species. The olfactory bulb is the part of the brain where the sense of smell is located; the OBR measures the proportion of the brain devoted to smell. Out of the 150 bird species where the OBR is known, the kakapo features as having one of the larger. Birds with standout OBRs include the kiwi and the snow petrel, the former well known for its facility for digging out worms and the latter a well-known navigator for whom a highly honed sense of smell may be vital in finding the snowbound burrow it nested in the previous season. It is also no coincidence that the kiwi and kakapo are nocturnal, and so likely rely on scent cues more than sight.

Julie speculates that where there are no mammal predators, island species may have evolved to be more highly scented than their mainland counterparts. Hawaiian honeycreepers and petrels are just some of the island birds that give off a musky odour: 'I think it is plausible that island birds may actually use self-produced odours more frequently (as social or sexual signals) than mainland species. We are just now realising that many or all birds have a functional sense of smell, and odours are widespread. All other vertebrates use odours to communicate, so why not birds?'

She notes that blue ducks produce pungent faeces, leaving them on the tops of rocks, almost like foxes and other vertebrates mark their territories. 'So, I suspect that scent is just another unusual trait that is free to evolve in mammal-free areas, just like ground nesting, flightlessness, and gigantism. Now that introduced mammals are in New Zealand, they probably can sniff out their prey fairly easily, especially if the bird has a strong scent like the kakapo [and is prone to "freezing" in the face of danger, like the kakapo],' says Julie.

Kakapo state house. These were a lot more convenient to work with than the deep burrows that kakapo sometimes favour as nests.

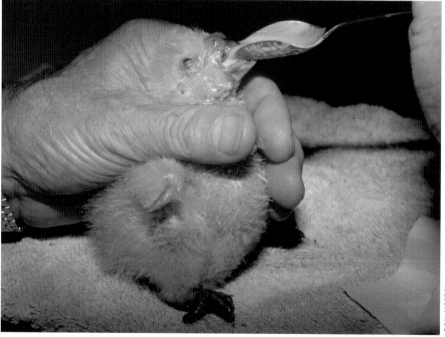

Spoon-feeding an 11-day-old nestling at Burwood Bush near Te Anau.

DON MERTON

Without the boost from supplementary foods, kakapo would have failed to achieve satisfactory breeding weights. Too much weight gain, though, may have been a factor in an excessive number of males being hatched compared to females, an issue addressed with careful targeted diets.

# Gender bias

By 1998 the kakapo population had risen to 57, of which 36 were male and 21 female. This male bias was a puzzle. One theory held that predators were more likely to kill females than males because of their vulnerability while nesting and feeding their young. The fact that all 18 of the Fiordland birds discovered in the 1970s were male seemed to support this notion. However, scientists who had studied the question of sex allocation proposed an alternative explanation. They contended that females in better condition should produce more offspring of the sex that shows the greater benefit from the improved condition. Because male kakapo fight each other for the attentions of females, and because they grow faster and larger than females, then according to the theory, mothers in good condition should produce more sons.

Sure enough, during the 1990s females whose diets were boosted with nuts and fruit hatched more male chicks than female – by an average of 67 per cent against 29 per cent for those not given extra food. This theory would prove important when the kakapo finally bred as exuberantly as they did in 2002.

When scientist Graeme Elliott spotted the first signs of a developing bumper fruit crop on Codfish rimu in early 2001, he recognised it as the precursor to a major mast fruiting year in 2002. Banking everything on this long-awaited event, the kakapo team swung into action. Elliott and team manager Paul Jansen decided to take the gamble of shifting all the adult females from Maud Island. By now all the birds had also been removed from Little Barrier because of their poor breeding performance there. All 21 females of breeding age were on Codfish by April 2001.

Monitoring equipment was brought in and volunteers or 'nest minders' were sought. In all, more than 100 people from Canada, Germany, Japan, the USA and the UK lent their time to the task between January and May 2002. Armed with the new scientific insights about the role of supplementary food in skewing the sex ratio, Elliott says the team had to perform a subtle balancing act. 'We had to provide enough food so that the birds reached the threshold for breeding but not so much that they'd put on too much weight,' he says. The strategy appears to have paid off. Of the 24 new kakapo in 2002, 15 (62 per cent) were female. Suddenly the sex ratio had shifted, so that now 41 individuals or 47 per cent of the total population were female.

Elaborate precautions were brought into play to ensure the safety of the eggs and chicks. As soon as a female laid an egg, nest watchers set up camp around 60 metres away, rigging up an infra-red warning system which signalled whenever the female left the nest. Immediately she did, the watchers moved in with a miniature video camera which was installed inside the nest cavity to monitor events over the next four months.

Don Merton says data loggers show the environment inside a kakapo nest resembles a butter cooler. Surrounded by saturated peat, the nests maintain a constant temperature of around 10°C, with humidity of between 98–100 per cent. In eight instances, the kakapo team built and transferred nests into nest boxes – 'kakapo state houses on the hillsides' in Elliott's words – to better protect nests from the elements (especially flooding) as well as to make it easier and safer to weigh eggs and chicks.

Don Merton is a master of egg manipulation. He moved fertile eggs from nests, replacing infertile ones in other nests, and gave the successful female another chance to lay another clutch. Because hatching is staggered at around two-day intervals, the last egg laid in a nest often hatches about six days after the first, and the chick fails to survive due to competition from older siblings. He and colleagues therefore moved eggs around so that each brood contained eggs of a similar age, and so that no female had more eggs and chicks than she could readily cope with.

For Don Merton, the 2002 breeding season was the breakthrough he and others had been waiting for. Among the many highlights of the season:

- Of the 26 hatchlings, 15 were female, lifting the female proportion of the population to 47 per cent;
- Hoki, the 10-year-old hand-reared kakapo from Maud Island, proved that birds

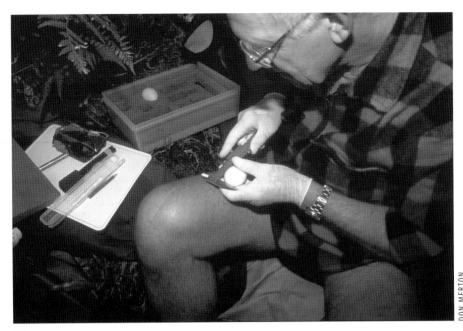

DON MERTON

■ Don Merton measures a kakapo egg.

could return to the wild and breed successfully. Although her fertile egg died during incubation, she was given a replacement, which she hatched and raised;

- Forty-one of the 86 birds are of known age, around 23 years or less. This is the reverse of the 1980s when the ages of most birds were not known but it was presumed many were elderly. The fact that half of the kakapo today are 23 years old or less means that in kakapo terms they are young, providing hope for the future of the species. Kakapo, it seems, can live at least as long as humans;

- Some kakapo bred without human assistance, ignoring the food handouts. Instead of being reliant on people for its survival, the kakapo has shown that it is capable of independence on Codfish Island;

- Even the oldest females, which may be more than 50, produced chicks, proving that old birds can breed to a ripe old age.

## And what of the future?

According to Graeme Elliott, 'everything kicks in 10 years from now'. If the 15 females hatched in 2002 are still alive in 2012, they will start to breed, and from that time on there ought to be an exponential increase in the population.

Welcome as that projection is, it poses its own problems. First there's the question of where the kakapo will live. Even though the 2002 bumper breeding year happened on Codfish Island, it appears that a major, successful rimu masting year might occur there only once every 20–25 years. While this is likely to be sufficient to cover losses in such a long-lived bird, there is then the problem of the kakapo outgrowing its island home. Each kakapo lives alone and needs a lot of space – 15–50 hectares of real estate for its home range. At 1396 hectares, Codfish is likely to become cramped for kakapo space in the near future with fewer than 100 birds. However, such a small population is unlikely to be genetically viable.

One option – in fact the only large mammal-free island currently available – is subantarctic Campbell Island, where rats have recently been exterminated. Campbell's area of 11,300 hectares might be able to accommodate several hundred kakapo, and, cool as it is compared to lowland New Zealand (averaging just 635 hours of annual sunshine, relatively low rainfall but 325 rain-days a year, and 6°C mean annual temperature), the cold-adapted parrot would find it no cooler in winter than subalpine Fiordland.

In 1998, for the first time, kakapo bred in pine forest. The female lived on pine needles from which she extracted the nutrients before discarding the "chews".

DON MERTON

Some of the 100 plus kakapo nest minders who volunteered their services for the historic 2002 breeding season on Codfish Island.

But Elliott has a slightly different vision of the future, albeit one where the kakapo would remain dependent on people: 'The subantarctics are a possibility, but it's not where they used to live. I have a dream to have them back on the mainland, probably Fiordland, but that's going to involve better technology than we have at present to control rats, cats, stoats and possums, and perhaps a fence like that surrounding Wellington's Karori Sanctuary.'

In July 2004 three juvenile kakapo transferred to Te Kakahu (Chalky) Island died from a soil bacterium, bringing the population down to eighty-three. The three birds were all two-year-old females. They were placed on the island in the hope that a beech seed masting year might encourage breeding.

## References

Clout, Mick N., and Merton, Don V., 'Saving the kakapo: the conservation of the world's most peculiar parrot', *Bird Conservation International* (1998), 8:281–96.

Clout, Mick N., Elliott, Graeme P., Robertson, Bruce C., 'Effects of supplementary feeding on the offspring sex ratio of kakapo: a dilemma for the conservation of a polygynous parrot', *Biological Conservation* (2002), 107: 13–18.

Cockrem, J. F., 'Reproductive biology and conservation of the endangered kakapo (*Strigops habroptilus*) in New Zealand', Proceedings of the International Congress on Bird Reproduction, Tours, September 1999, 139–44.

Hagelin, Julie, 'Observations on the olfactory ability of the kakapo *Strigops habroptilus*, the critically endangered parrot of New Zealand', *Ibis* (2004), 146: 161–64.

# Parea

*Handsome pigeon
of the island forest*

| | |
|---|---|
| Scientific name | *Hemiphaga novaeseelandiae chathamensis* |
| Popular name | parea, Chatham Island pigeon |
| Conservation status | protected nationally critical endemic |
| Population | 150+ (in 2004) |
| Where found | Tuku-a-Tamatea River, Chatham Island; Pitt and South East islands |
| Life span | up to 25 years |
| Size | 800 g; 55 cm |
| Breeding | June–October; most breed at 1–2 years |
| Nest sites | a platform of sticks or a tangle of vines in a tree |
| Clutch size | 1 egg |
| Feeding | fruits of hoho, matipo, mahoe and karamu, and foliage of mahoe, hoho and clover |
| Behaviour | spectacular flying dives, especially by the males, to attract a mate |

What a difference a bit of predator trapping and time makes. In the late 1980s the parea or Chatham Island pigeon was down to about 40 birds and the countdown to extinction had begun. But by 1994 numbers had bounced back to 150 individuals, and today there are probably close to two hundred and fifty. 'For a while it was rarer than the kakapo!' exclaims DOC's Graeme Taylor.

But unlike the kakapo, the black robin or the takahe, the parea is not a household name. That disregard stems largely from its status: adjudged a subspecies of the mainland pigeon, the parea has therefore had few resources directed at it compared to birds considered full species. Soon, though, the scientific community might accord the parea the standing it deserves.

Difficult as it might be to believe today, the parea was once 'extraordinarily abundant', inhabiting Chatham, Pitt, South East (Rangatira) and Mangere islands. Plentiful fossil remains support anecdotal evidence that the birds were widespread. According to scientists Ian Atkinson and Phil Millener, subfossil bones of parea have been found more frequently than bones of any other forest bird in dune deposits on Chatham Island. Today the parea is found on its stronghold of Chatham Island, but there are also a few on Pitt Island and South East Island.

Moriori, who settled the Chathams 500–600 years ago, hunted the parea with relatively low-tech weapons such as spears and captured them in snares, but it was the arrival of Europeans in the early 1800s, and later Maori, that signalled the beginning of the large-scale decline. Not only did they burn forests for farmland, they also introduced possums, cats, rats and pigs, which either ate the forest habitat, or the birds themselves. Given the chance, possums will eat almost anything, including eggs and chicks in the nest. The weka, introduced from the South Island in 1905, is also presumed to be a predator. The forest clearance not only deprived the birds of food and their habitat, it also led to an upsurge in the numbers of the Australasian harrier, which eats parea eggs and chicks.

Unused to such predators, over thousands of years the parea developed risky habits like nesting on the ground, or just above it, making them easy prey for weka. Cattle or sheep are also more likely to damage a nest at ground level. But not all parea nest on the ground; a study carried out between 1991 and 1994 of 101 nests found most perched about four metres up a tree. Here they were vulnerable to cats, ship rats, possums and harriers.

By the 1980s, the parea had largely retreated to a forested area of around 400 hectares in the south-west corner of Chatham Island, including the catchments of the Awatotara Creek, Tuku-a-Tamatea River, Kawhaki Creek and Waipurua Creek. This forest was also the home of the elusive petrel, the taiko. Concerned at the

IAN FLUX, DOC

■ Between 1991 and 1994, 27 adult pigeons were caught using mist nets and then monitored to learn about their behaviour and feeding and breeding habits.

J. L. KENDRICK, DOC

A mosaic of valleys, ridges and plateaus, the parea area in the Awatotara and Tuku catchments is recovering from decades of pest infestation. Fencing, trapping and replanting are helping to bring about rapid restoration.

dwindling population, in 1983 Wildlife Service staff tried to relocate 13 parea from southern Chatham Island to South East. It was a forlorn hope: some of the birds died in transit and only one pair attempted to breed but they were unsuccessful.

In 1984, Manuel and Evelyn Tuanui donated 1012 hectares of their land to protect the two rare species in what is now called the Tuku Nature Reserve. In order to improve the taiko's prospects of survival, part of the area was fenced in 1985 to stop stock wandering in. Son Bruce Tuanui and his wife Liz supplemented the Tuku Reserve by covenanting 200 hectares of adjoining forest land; using money from the Nature Heritage Fund and DOC, these areas of open forest were fenced in 1992–93. Cats, rats and possums were targeted from 1989, principally to protect the taiko, but the parea soon began to benefit as well.

Scientist Dr Ralph Powlesland arrived in the Tuku Reserve in 1991, heading a four-man team which would spend periods of the next three years intensively

DOC

Scientist Ralph Powlesland, who led the research into the parea, holds a juvenile. Following predator control on the Chathams, parea breeding success stood at 68 per cent, compared to 22 per cent for kereru on the mainland.

# Pecking order

To most of us the question of whether an animal is a full species or a subspecies is academic, but in reality the answer has important consequences. Government and other agencies often prioritise their spending on conservation according to whether an animal or plant is a full species or subspecies, on the grounds that the full species is more genetically distinct and therefore more worthy of saving from extinction.

In the past, taxonomists based their decisions on whether to grant an animal or plant the accolade of a full species by such things as appearance and ecology. Their verdicts are now assisted by DNA evidence, which is particularly useful when looking at animals or plants that appear similar. So, for example, in New Zealand a rash of 'new' gecko species have turned up in the last decade, simply because new techniques have enabled taxonomists to split the forest gecko and common gecko into at least 13 different species.

■ During spring the parea spends a lot of time feeding on the grass. Such habits leave it at the mercy of predators.

The Chatham Island pigeon is clearly related to the kereru or mainland pigeon, but because the Chathams have been separated from the mainland for so long the parea has evolved in ways quite distinct from its mainland relative. However, such sharp-eyed early European ornithologists such as Dieffenbach, Buller and Travers, who visited the Chathams between 1840 and 1871, failed to observe any differences. It was not until 1891 that W. Rothschild described it as a full species – *Hemiphaga chathamensis*. He noted: 'It is one-fifth larger than *Hemiphaga novaeseelandiae* and is purple and pearl grey where the latter is green and bronze red.' Others agreed with Rothschild that the plumage of the parea set it apart from the mainland species and gave it full species status.

But the parea's day in the sun as a full-blown species did not last long; by 1970 it was downgraded to a subspecies and has remained there until the present day. However, thanks to scientists Dr Phil Millener and Dr Ralph Powlesland, the parea will most likely become a full species again, if a recently published paper gets widely accepted. In it they argue that while the plumage, greater size and heavier bill of the parea have been mentioned no scientists have compared the bone structure of the two pigeon species.

Millener, a New Zealander now living in the United States, used the resources of Washington's National Museum of Natural History to analyse the parea's size and the proportions of its bones compared to the mainland kereru. The analysis shows that the parea was possibly heading down the road to flightlessness. Not only is it heavier than the kereru, but it has also evolved features such as less curved claws and an enlarged hind toe – a possible precursor to enable it to ultimately scrabble about on the forest floor. Already the parea nests as low as a metre above the ground, one of the reasons for its vulnerability.

Yet the parea is still an accomplished flier and glider. In 1893 H. O. Forbes, then director of the Canterbury Museum, was delighted to watch the pigeon which 'loves to play in the strong up-current that towers in the air, rebounding from the perpendicular face of the cliffs, when a strong sea-breeze is blowing'.

Other features separate the kereru and the parea: the parea generally nests in June–October, the kereru in September–January; the parea nests in bracken or fern near the ground even when there is a tree available (unlike the kereru which keeps higher and as much out of harm's way as possible); and the parea's single egg is significantly larger than that of the kereru.

The robust bill of the parea allows the bird to tear at and eat mature, leathery hoho leaves; by comparison, the kereru has not been observed eating the foliage of the hoho's mainland relative, the lancewood.

Another key difference between the kereru and the parea is the distance each flies. On the mainland the pigeon is prepared to fly up to 18 kilometres from its home base to find food, including across the ocean. The parea, by contrast, rarely makes flights of more than five kilometres; although, because there are few food sources beyond the core area where they live, there is not an incentive for them to fly far.

studying the parea. It soon became clear that food supply was the key to how well they bred. Whereas on the mainland the kereru has the choice of a wide variety of plants, from miro to kahikatea to tawa, on the Chathams many of these types of plants with large fruits are missing. The parea's favoured foods are hoho, a lancewood (*Pseudopanax chathamicus*), kopi (*Corynocarpus laevigatus*), lacebark (*Plagianthus betulinus* var. *chathamicus*), matipo (*Myrsine chathamica*), supplejack (*Ripogonum scandens*) and karamu (*Coprosma chathamica*).

Bulky material such as leaves form a significant portion of the parea's diet, which also helps account for its larger size and its more robust bill, which is useful for tearing off the hoho's tough mature leaves. The study revealed that the succulent fruits of the hoho are especially sought after by the parea. These are at their best in August and September, coinciding with the peak of the pigeon's breeding season, but are also available as early as June and as late as December.

The importance of having the right food, and good quantities of it, were brought home during the study. Even though the start of the breeding season in July matched the coldest time of the year, parea parents were able to successfully raise a chick from the one egg laid. In addition, the female was then likely to lay another egg, and in exceptional years a third. By starting early and having ample supplies of food, the parea could stretch the breeding season out.

The overall nesting success of the parea was 68 per cent during the course of the study – a much better rate than for mainland pigeons where there was no predator control. At four areas on the mainland studied between 1984–93, the best nesting success was 22 per cent, and at two of the areas, no pigeons were able to breed. The conclusion is inescapable: get rid of the predators and pigeon numbers will increase.

A further factor in the parea's favour was its survival rate. During the study period, nearly 90 per cent of nestlings reached one year of age. The combination of all these factors meant that by 1994 the number of adult parea had tripled to 120, and the bird was out of the extinction danger zone. Like a number of New Zealand's endangered species, the parea is relatively long-lived, so conservation managers have the luxury of time on their side. Life expectancy of the birds is 24.5 years.

Graeme Taylor, who keeps an eye on the parea while carrying out taiko work, believes parea numbers could increase to 400–600 birds, if secure forests could be found for them. As the population increases, juveniles are flying further from their birthplace to set up home in forests which are not protected. 'The only way for numbers to really expand is more pest control outside the Tuku catchment. It would be best to predator-proof some of the new covenants on main Chatham Island,' says Graeme.

GRAEME TAYLOR

A plump parea chick on the nest. Nestlings fledge at about 45 days old and become independent at three months.

Already Chatham Islanders are getting used to seeing pigeons in areas outside the Tuku Reserve. Not only does that kindle their interest in the parea's fate, it also suggests that the pigeon is carrying out the vital work of spreading seed and thus creating habitable areas beyond the confines of the reserves.

## References

*Parea Recovery Plan*, Department of Conservation, 2001.

Flux, I. A., Powlesland, R. G., Dilks, P. J., and Grant, A. D., 'Breeding, survival and recruitment of the Chatham Island pigeon (*Hemiphaga chathamensis*)', *Notornis* (2001), 48: 177–206.

Grant, A. D., Powlesland, R. G., Dilks, P. J., Flux, I. A., and Tisdall, C. J., 'Mortality, distribution, numbers and conservation of the Chatham Island pigeon (*Hemiphaga novaeseelandiae chathamensis*)', *Notornis* (1997), 44: 65–77.

Millener, P. R., and Powlesland, R. G., 'The Chatham Islands pigeon (Parea) deserves full species status: *Hemiphaga chathamensis*' (Rothschild; Aves: Columbidae. *Journal of the Royal Society of New Zealand*, June 2001, Vol. 31, No. 2: 365–83.

# 7 Rowi

## *Rare ratite of the Okarito forests*

| | |
|---:|:---|
| Scientific name | *Apteryx rowi* |
| Popular name | rowi |
| Conservation status | protected nationally critically endemic |
| Population | 200+ (in 2004) |
| Where found | Okarito |
| Life span | 40–60 years |
| Size | 2.2 kg (male), 2.8 kg (female); 40 cm |
| Breeding | June–December |
| Nest sites | burrows |
| Clutch size | 1 egg; a massive 430 g in weight |
| Feeding | worms, larvae of beetles, cicadas, spiders, weta, crickets, centipedes |
| Behaviour | nocturnal, high-pitched whistler, sexes share incubation |

The view from the Okarito trig, stretching from the pounding coast through lowland podocarp and broadleaf rainforest to foothills and encompassing the lofty summits of Aoraki (Mt Cook) and Mt Tasman, is as sublime as anywhere in the world. But today Jo Crofton has not come to admire the outlook. The DOC ranger is on the trail of one of the 200 Okarito kiwi in the 10,000-hectare area that is their home. Bounded on the north by the Okarito River, on the south by the fast-flowing Waiho River which disgorges out of the Franz Josef Glacier, and by State Highway 6 to the east, the geographically well-defined sanctuary houses the rarest kiwi in the world.

'Rowi', as the bird is known to the local runanga, Te Runanga o Makaawhio, is also the latest kiwi to be scientifically described. Once regarded as simply the Okarito brown kiwi, a southern relative of the more common North Island brown, it has now been accepted as a separate species with its own unique scientific name: *Apteryx rowi*.

Sid Marsh, who has worked with kiwi throughout New Zealand since 1992 and at Okarito for three years, characterises the rowi as a particularly social animal. 'They are more intelligent than people realise, forming tight, interactive family groups. They are very gregarious creatures with an innate curiosity, not only of other rowi but also of humans. Extended family members live together – in one long-term breeding burrow I've seen Mum, Dad, teenage daughter (aged about 18 months),

# **Rowi** and the **sound** of **silence**

Dr Hugh Robertson, Bank of New Zealand kiwi recovery science coordinator, believes the Okarito rowi population has never been much greater than 1–2000 birds in historical times, unlike the North Island brown kiwi which numbered in the millions. He contends that the rowi has been confined to the forests just south of Okarito since at least the late 1800s, when Charlie Douglas recorded them only from exactly the same area which they inhabit nowadays. To the south flows the natural boundary of the Waiho River which would thwart any migration in that direction. But the northern and eastern boundaries are less of an obstacle to movement. So why does the rowi prefer to stay in one place?

'I think that these kiwi fear a kiwi silence. In other words, they don't like to go to areas where there are no other kiwi calling. It's a mechanism to keep them within their own kind,' says Robertson. In this, the rowi's behaviour differs from that of the North Island brown kiwi. A young male rowi elects to remain within the sanctuary and will fight with an adult kiwi for

IRENE PETROV

■ The tiny rowi chick Namu fitted with a transmitter just after being caught. Distinctive creamy head patches show up clearly in this image.

territory. By contrast, the brown kiwi disperses far and wide from its birthplace in order to stake a territorial claim.

Other characteristics also set the rowi apart. It looks slightly different to the brown kiwi, with soft and slightly greyish plumage, sometimes complemented by cream facial feathers. Compared to the brown kiwi it is soft to the touch rather than coarse.

The rowi's style of parenting is also in contrast to that of the brown kiwi, but the same as the Stewart Island kiwi (tokoeka) and the great spotted kiwi. Both male and female rowi take turns to look after the egg on the nest, whereas with the brown kiwi the male performs this task. Once the chick is hatched, juvenile rowi remain with the parents for at least six months; brown kiwi juveniles are on their own after just 10–50 days. In fact, one young rowi female was found keeping her parents company three and a half years after hatching, although she had left the parental burrow for a time before returning. Some Stewart Island tokoeka have an even stronger attachment to family. One female was still with her parents seven years after hatching.

toddler (three-week-old chick), and an egg. I think their breeding burrows might have been used for generations.

'They have well-worn kiwi runs to and from the main entrance and inside there can sometimes be bucketloads of dry cosy-looking leaf litter heaped up, behind which one can sometimes just see Mum and Dad's respective heads popping up to look outwards. Once or twice a year the birds spring-clean by kicking out old litter and shell, and bringing in new dry crispy stuff, which they mound up just outside the entrance. A good many of these home burrows are in what we call 'fortress logs' – hollowed out southern rata trunks which are often covered in moss.' says Marsh.

Crofton tells me to be prepared for a demanding trudge across country to where his quarry is in hiding. Fortunately the rain that the West Coast is renowned for has only fallen briefly during the past few weeks. In this sort of country, leather tramping boots are an expensive waste which rapidly rot, he explains; the preferred DOC footwear is rubber gumboots.

As we make our way through the bush, Crofton brings me up to date with efforts to save the species from extinction. It was only in the early 1990s that attention began to be paid to the plight of the kiwi in general, and rowi in particular. For a long time New Zealanders had become complacent about the ability of the kiwi to survive, but several events occurred to challenge this attitude. One was the horrifying tale of a German shepherd let loose in Northland's Waitangi State Forest in 1987 which slaughtered perhaps 500 kiwi in a few weeks.

Then in the late 1980s, DOC scientists picked up on a worrying trend: North Island brown kiwi were starting to disappear, chief among the culprits were ferrets which had been released by farmers when the bottom fell out of the ferret fur industry. Concern about the fate of the kiwi gathered momentum, culminating in the Bank of New Zealand taking the national bird under its wing in 1991 with a multi-million-dollar pledge to support a recovery programme.

Now the spotlight shone on the kiwi, and nowhere was its beam more intense than at Okarito. Although the Okarito population was not considered a species in its own right at the time, some scientists had a hunch that it might be. Initial surveys of the forest showed that there might have been as few as 50 birds, but fresh surveys in successive years kept turning up more. The consensus today is that numbers had dropped to about 150 and that the species was on a downward course. 'We knew that the population of rowi was falling because of predators, and that we had to do something quickly to stop its decline. We identified stoats as the main problem, with possums and dogs as the other major predators at this site, so we began to target them,' says Crofton.

DOC

■ Irene Petrov with Beegee, a 520-gram rowi chick rescued from the forest during the 2000–2001 breeding season.

That list has been altered as more has been discovered. Possums, which have been captured on videotape entering rowi burrows and have also been implicated in the direct killing of other native wildlife, either by eating eggs or chicks, have not been a great menace to rowi since their numbers were reduced to a low level by a very successful aerial 1080 poison operation in 1998.

More problematic is the question of a lowland population of the alpine parrot, the kea, which breeds in the Okarito sanctuary, and has been observed to eat rowi eggs. As a native bird in fairly low numbers, the kea's future also has to be safeguarded. Because it was believed that kea might follow humans to rowi burrows, the people working with the kiwi have become more circumspect around nests. The cautious approach appears to have paid off, with fewer attacks in recent years.

# Charlie Douglas and the kiwi

**Westland explorer Charlie Douglas was a harsh critic of the kiwi – a view at odds with today's more affectionate regard for the national bird. Here are some choice quotes from a monograph he wrote in 1899 called *Birds of South Westland*.**

The kiwi is certainly not of high type. It looks like a being one would expect to see in the moon, Mars, or some dying out Planet. When running about in the moonlight, it looks like a ghost of a bird, espicially [*sic*] if it has just been digging in a rotton [ *sic*] log, when its beak is often luminous.

It is in captivity that their dense stupidity can best be seen. If put in a room, they will go tramping around close to the wall using their beaks as a walking stick. If a box or a tub with water in it, is put against the wall, he doesn't go round, but if possible climbs into the tub, through the water, and so on for hours, never thinking to avoid the tub and water, if he can get round the back of the fire so much the better. Never mind a singeing.

As for eating a kiwi. Just before they commence breeding they are very fat and good eating. Still I must confess it requires some considerable practice to get the acquired taste. They have an earthy flavour, which to many would be disagreeable. The best definition I ever heard about roast or boiled kiwi, was a man, remarking it tasted as he should imagine a piece of pork boiled in an old coffin would be like.

Altogether the kiwi, excep [*sic*] in a museum . . . is of neither use nor ornament. His intelligence is about on the same level as a spider, and it seems almost impossible to develop it. No doubt like every living thing, it has its uses in creation, but as his work is done in the dark, it is not apparent enough for people to give him any credit for it.

Although they do not kill rowi, European rats may also pose problems, 'hoovering' up insects and invertebrates, which are the rowi's major food, and so potentially affect breeding because the adult rowi are not in robust enough condition. Rats also disturb wildlife, possibly putting them on edge and under stress. When the first chicks were hatched during 2003, following heavy rat infestations, they were six weeks later than usual, and the parents were underweight.

# Trapping programme

In 2000 the Government provided a major boost to a number of endangered wildlife programmes, among them the rowi. This enabled DOC staff in 2001 to launch the largest stoat-trapping programme in the world – of course, nowhere in the world do these introduced mustelids (the family which includes ferrets and weasels) pose such a problem to native wildlife as they do in New Zealand. They set up 250 kilometres of trap lines with about 1500 tunnels, in each of which were two traps baited with hen's eggs.

SID MARSH

■ Grisly find: a 702-gram rowi juvenile that had just been killed and stashed in a stoat den four to five hours before kiwi worker Sid Marsh discovered it. The wily stoat had managed to avoid being ensnared in the tunnel trap baited with an egg.

SID MARSH

■ Hera Smith weighs a rowi sub-adult, February 2003.

The payoff was immediate, with 446 stoats caught by February 2002. To test the effectiveness of the trapping operation, all kiwi chicks were left in the forest to fend for themselves. The verdict: the operation was a success. Chick survival rate is normally only five per cent, but in the 2001–2002 season it rose to 30 per cent. Of the 20 chicks that were fitted with transmitters, 14 died, 12 of those because of stoats. 'But we were pleased to see that six of the chicks survived past one kilogram, by which stage they were pretty well immune to stoat attacks. This was the first significant natural recruitment since the programme began and represented a major turning point. It showed that the stoat-control operation was at least partially successful,' says Crofton.

The rowi team was encouraged to continue with a hands-off policy for the following season. However, nature had its own plans. The summer of 2001–2002 was a rimu 'mast' season, an extraordinarily heavy fruiting year for the stately podocarp. In 30 years of monitoring the forests, ecologists had not witnessed such fertility. Rats were the first to take advantage of the profusion of food. As day follows night, stoat numbers leapt, feasting on the abundance of rats. But they were not particular about what they ate, and consequently rowi chicks also found themselves on the menu. Despite the barrage of traps, sufficient numbers of stoats invaded the sanctuary to put kiwi chicks at risk. By early January 2003, all 14 monitored chicks were dead, and stoats were chiefly to blame.

And then, against the usual predictions, rats did not disappear during the winter of 2003. This time the kahikatea, another podocarp, exploded into fruit and the rats persisted through the winter. To give an indication of the scale of the invasion, during November 2001, 117 rats were caught; by October 2002 the number had increased to 801; and by October 2003, the rat plague was so great that 1610 were trapped. At the same time, the number of stoats killed during successive Decembers in 2001, 2002 and 2003 rose from 25 to 139, peaking at three hundred and thirty-one. It was time to reactivate the successful Operation Nest Egg programme that had been placed in abeyance for several seasons.

# Operation Nest Egg

Operation Nest Egg (ONE) began in 1994 as an answer to the problem of chicks being killed by ferrets, stoats or cats. Studies have shown that by the time a kiwi reaches 1000 grams in weight, it is capable of looking after itself. Therefore, eggs are taken from burrows and placed into a number of hatcheries around the country; the chicks are released once the risky juvenile period is over. Newly hatched chicks are also rescued and, in the case of the rowi, are relocated to a kiwi crèche on Motuara

SID MARSH

■ An adult rowi nestled in among a kiwi worker's kit, just before a transmitter change.

Island in the Marlborough Sounds until they are ready to return to the wild.

According to Bank of New Zealand kiwi recovery science coordinator Hugh Robertson, ONE has given the kiwi and conservation managers 'breathing space, because it has increased rowi numbers by about 25 per cent since 1995 to about 200 today. ONE demands that we have transmitters on the birds in perpetuity because that is the easiest way of tracking eggs and chicks, [but this] is not ideal in the long term because it benefits only kiwi in the ecosystem, not the whole environment in which they've evolved over millions of years.'

Robertson says that as much as possible he is trying to avoid overt intervention.

# Complex ecology

**Like a game of chess, the dynamics of the ecology of a South Westland rainforest are endlessly complex. The moves that one or other of the players make might have unseen ramifications many years later. In the mission to save the rowi, Dr Hugh Robertson is trying to make sense of this intricate web of life.**

It is not as if there were never predators endangering the kiwi, he points out. The extinct giant eagle (*Hapagornis*) and the laughing owl both inhabited the area and were skilled twilight or night-time killers. Harriers still kill Northland kiwi today, and extinct adzebills and current-day weka have always had an opportunistic eye for a meal. But today in South Westland, wily stoats have become enemy number one.

By becoming largely nocturnal, kiwi avoided many predators; another clue that they have had to be on their guard against marauders is the fact that kiwi camouflage their nests before heading off to forage.

Following a major poisoning operation in late 1998, possum numbers have dropped, but their departure, coupled with the rimu mast season of 2001–2002, has complicated matters. With no competition for food from possums, and intensive stoat trapping reducing numbers of their main predator, ship rats multiplied out of control. Normally winter and wet weather puts paid to rats, but during the winter of 2003 lactating females continued to be caught. By nature secretive animals, they were so abundant that they could be spotted in the bush during the day. 'This showed us that controlling stoats alone may do funny things to the ecosystem,' says Robertson.

Up until then Robertson had been hoping to avoid using 1080 poison in the sanctuary because this extra intervention would complicate matters further. Another reason was that it was unreliable to depend on poisons, since in some years operations had to be cancelled because of poor weather. One of the expected outcomes of using 1080 would be to kill rats and also a secondary kill of any stoats living in the sanctuary which were shy of traps. But since

About 120 of the birds have transmitters on them and it is a massive job to change them once a year. He acknowledges that it has been thanks to ONE that rowi numbers have increased to their present levels but more is yet to be done to ensure their long-term survival.

## References

*Kiwi (Apteryx* spp.*) recovery plan, 1996–2006*, Department of Conservation, 2003.
Burbridge, M. L., Colbourne, R. M., Robertson, H. A., and Baker, A. J., 'Molecular and other biological evidence supports the recognition of at least three species of brown kiwi', *Conservation Genetics* (2003), 4: 167–77.

many thousands of stoats are outside the sanctuary, a much larger area would have to be poisoned for maximum effect. That would entail technical problems and a large amount of money which could be better used for other kiwi work.

In the end, though, the DOC managers had to intervene. As much as anything, it became a question of politics. 'People demand success. They don't like it when they hear how all the chicks in one year have been taken by stoats, even though this might be perfectly acceptable from a population perspective in such a long-lived species – as long as productivity in the good years more than makes up the losses in these bad years. By intervening we may never learn whether our management works in the long term.'

And so at the beginning of 2003 when no chicks survived from that season, it was decided that any eggs and chicks that arrived after that date would be removed to safety. That left the Okarito team to deal with another problem: the rat plague. Should the rats be left to overpopulate the sanctuary and eat themselves out of house and home, leading to an eventual collapse of the population? Or should they be poisoned?

If recent anecdotal information of the impact of rats on Kapiti Island kiwi is anything to go by, then the rats may pose a significant threat. Since rats were eradicated from the island in the late 1990s, little spotted kiwi have gained weight. 'It might be that rats and kiwi are competing for the same foods. So down in Okarito the rats might starve themselves out, but they might also starve the kiwi out too,' suggests Robertson.

The Royal Forest and Bird Protection Society is a vocal proponent of the poison option. It points to times when 1080 poison has been dropped from helicopters: virtually all the stoats in forests have been killed by feeding on poisoned possums and rats.

For the moment though, that is a move that DOC has not made; however, with the removal of 13 rowi chicks to Motuara Island in early 2004, the impact of stoats has been checked temporarily. And who knows: continual refinements in conservation techniques might allow DOC managers to declare checkmate in the near future.

# Shore Plover

## *Beautiful shorebird of the Roaring Forties*

| | |
|---|---|
| **Scientific name** | *Thinornis novaeseelandiae* |
| **Popular names** | tuturuatu, shore plover |
| **Conservation status** | critically endangered endemic |
| **Population** | approximately 200 (in 2004) |
| **Where found** | South East Island, Mangere Island and an unidentified island off the North Island's east coast |
| **Life span** | 10–15 years, though the oldest known bird is 23 years old |
| **Size** | 50–60 g; 20 cm |
| **Breeding** | October–November; most breed at 2 years of age |
| **Nest sites** | bulky nests, well lined with vegetation, found beneath grasses, vines, boulders or piles of beach-wracked logs |
| **Clutch size** | 3 eggs |
| **Feeding** | crustaceans, molluscs, insects and their larvae |
| **Behaviour** | highly territorial when breeding, gregarious when not breeding |

For the ornithological romantic, New Zealand's offshore islands are still capable of coming up with surprises, decades after the door has supposedly closed on any fresh revelations. One recent example is that of the shore plover, a distinctive, lively shorebird once widespread throughout New Zealand but until lately known to survive only on South East Island (Rangatira), one of the smaller Chatham islands. It has been also recently reintroduced to an island off the coast of the North Island, using captive-bred birds.

Alison Davis, who has been keeping a close eye on the small birds since the mid-1980s, recalls the shock she received in 1999 when a colleague phoned her to let her know a new population of the shore plover had been discovered. 'I was completely blown away; I couldn't believe it, after all the years I'd spent working with them,' she says.

The intriguing feature of the hitherto unknown, 21-strong population was that it inhabited a storm-swept exposed reef called the Western Reef rising a few metres above sea level, and lying almost 100 kilometres distant from the main group of birds

MIKE BELL

■ Shaun O'Connor collects shore plover eggs from South East Island for transfer to Mt Bruce Wildlife Reserve, where they will be captive-reared and later released on to a secure island.

SHAUN O'CONNOR

■ Juvenile shore plovers are kept in this aviary on Mangere Island to acclimatise them to the environment and encourage them to regard the island as home. In the early 2000s, scores were released onto the island which has a limited habitat for the birds but is predator free.

on South East, where numbers have averaged about 130 since 1981. Although they can fly, shore plovers by nature like to stay in one place. They have what is called strong 'site fidelity'. Where could they have come from? 'I think they could have come from Rangatira, but it does seem a strange thing. To reach the Western Reef they would have had to fly over Pitt Island and main Chatham Island,' says Alison.

Surely such sedentary birds would choose to land on the large nearby islands, rather than continue flying to a tiny rocky outpost which in extreme weather is completely engulfed by large swells. Adding to the mystery is the fact that DNA testing revealed the Western Reef birds to be distinct from those on South East. The likely explanation is that the Western Reef birds are a physical and genetic remnant of the shore plover population that resided in the north-eastern end of main Chatham Island prior to the arrival of predators such as cats and weka, which then wiped them out from the main island. According to DOC's recovery plan for the shore plover, 'the tiny Western Reef population appears to have survived, undetected and completely separate from the Rangatira population, for a hundred years or more'.

Unfortunately the euphoria over the discovery was short-lived. Within a few years numbers had dwindled to one, possibly because of a hefty increase in the seal population on the reef that left little room for the plovers. Luckily, the last remaining

DON MERTON

Male shore plover, South East Island.

bird, a male dubbed Westy, was caught and transferred to the Mt Bruce Wildlife Centre in the Wairarapa. He subsequently produced an offspring in captivity in early 2004. The aim is to increase his unique genetic bloodline in captivity and produce enough birds for eventual return to a safe site back in the Chathams.

Elsewhere the plover recovery programme is showing every sign of being a success. 'The significant thing is that we have been able to establish another population, and this has been on an island off mainland New Zealand, where the shore plover was once abundant,' says Alison.

On the mainland, the plover's downfall came about with the arrival of rats, and later cats. Unlike most other shore-dwelling species, the plover breeds under thick vegetation, rather than the casual-looking scrape in the sand favoured by oystercatchers or dotterels. Predators are thus able to sneak up on the plover without being seen.

Scientists from Cook's 1773 expedition saw plovers in locations as far apart as Dusky Sound in Fiordland and Queen Charlotte Sound in the Marlborough Sounds, so it is assumed they were common throughout the country. Although people still recorded seeing them as late as the 1880s, these reports are considered doubtful, and no specimens could back up the claims. The last reliable mainland report came from the Waikawa River, Otago, in 1871.

SHAUN O'CONNOR

Conducting a shore plover census can be a difficult business. Young plovers blend in perfectly with their surroundings, and the coast is an obstacle course of slippery rocks and deep pools.

ROSE COLLEN

'Westy', the last survivor of a small shore plover population which lived in splendid isolation for more than 100 years on the eight-hectare Western Reef off the Chathams, was captured in 2003 and taken to the Mt Bruce Wildlife Centre where his valuable genes are being passed on to future shore plovers in the captive breeding programme.

SHAUN O'CONNOR

Unusually for plovers, the New Zealand variety nests under vegetation, sometimes more than 100 metres above the high-tide line. The heavily pigmented eggs take about 28 days to hatch.

That left the Chathams as the bird's only stronghold. Before long, cats exterminated them on Mangere and Pitt islands, but by some miracle neither cats nor rats set up camp on neighbouring South East Island. There the hardy little birds carried on, managing to survive despite the fact that collectors took hundreds of specimens for well-paying New Zealand and European clients.

Ornithologist Richard Sibson writes of the plunder: '. . . the incredible number of specimens in museums both local and overseas proves how eagerly these beautiful little plovers were sought after and what a good price they would fetch. Some of the collectors who took hundreds of specimens between 1890 and 1910 left their names carved on the rafters of the woolshed that was used as their base.'

Little was heard of the shore plover again until 1937 when Charles Fleming and Graham Turbott made their historic visit to the Chathams. As they feared, they saw no birds on Mangere and Pitt islands, but on South East they found 'a thriving population' of an estimated 52 pairs of plovers.

By the 1970s numbers had dropped to between an estimated 68 and 90 birds, partly because with the removal of sheep in 1961, natural vegetation was regrowing, depriving the plover of the cleared areas it uses above the coastline (dubbed 'The Clears'). Concerned by this decline, the Wildlife Service moved some birds to Mangere Island (by then cleared of cats) in the early 1980s. However, the plovers displayed an unerring homing instinct and in short order returned to South East or simply disappeared. In one transfer attempt, they managed to beat the boat that had ferried them to Mangere back to South East. Even when their primary feathers were removed and wing feathers clipped, they failed to establish on Mangere. They simply waited three months for the feathers to grow back before heading for home.

Department of Conservation staff again attempted to reintroduce them to Mangere in 2001. This time they used only juvenile birds that had just fledged and held them in an aviary for up to a month on Mangere before release – a technique described as 'soft release'. It was hoped the juveniles would not have formed a homing association with South East, and by holding them in an aviary they had a chance to settle down after the stress of handling and transfer, and be well fed before release. Three transfers of between 13 and 15 juveniles were undertaken annually from 2001–2003, and each time the birds were held in the aviary before release.

Although some of the birds returned to South East, pairs formed and bred on Mangere each summer after they were liberated. In the summer of 2003–2004 the new population on Mangere stood at 14 birds, including at least three pairs and two juveniles fledged on the island. No more releases are planned; with luck the population will generate its own head of steam and become self-sustaining.

Despite the earlier Mangere setback in the 1980s, Alison Davis still held out hopes for establishing another wild population as a safeguard against extinction. The National Wildlife Centre at Mt Bruce and the Isaac Wildlife Trust near Christchurch were chosen as captive rearing facilities. Techniques for hatching the eggs, raising the chicks and forming a captive population took some time, but it is now a 'well-oiled' programme according to recovery group leader for the shore plover, Shaun O'Connor. However, launching a third population has proven to be quite another proposition.

Between 1994 and 2000, 75 shore plovers were released onto Motuora Island in the Hauraki Gulf. By the end of the 1999–2000 breeding season, only one breeding pair was still on the island. The remainder had simply flown away and presumably died in the hostile environment they found themselves in, or they had been killed by moreporks that lived on the island. The latter was unexpected, says Alison Davis. 'The fact that moreporks had killed some of the plovers came completely out of the blue. We thought to ourselves, surely to God a few moreporks aren't going to wipe out the population, but that is in fact what they did,' she says.

If moreporks did not actually kill all the shore plovers, they probably chased the

SHAUN O'CONNOR

Attaching a transmitter to a shore plover, South East Island.

SHAUN O'CONNOR

Chicks are banded so they can be easily recognised. The rings are sealed with glue so there are no gaps where pieces of grit might work their way behind the rings, causing injury.

DON MERTON

■ Kiwi conservation ingenuity: to protect the nests of burrowing birds from clumsy feet, workers wear these 'burrow boards' attached with snowboard bindings.

remainder off the island. Just why shore plovers should be susceptible to morepork predation is uncertain. On the Chathams they co-exist with skuas which are often fiercely predatory, and in former times they would have lived side by side with moreporks on the mainland. The most likely explanation is that the captive-reared birds were not trained to recognise predators and thus fell prey to them.

Shaun O'Connor agrees that it never occurred to wildlife staff that moreporks would be a problem. 'There were five pairs of moreporks and very little for them to eat on the island. When the plovers arrived the moreporks must have thought it was Christmas,' he says. Some plovers which found themselves unwelcome on the island were discovered as far afield as Kaipara Harbour to the north-west and Whangamata to the south. Shaun says he pondered whether to control the moreporks or not. However, he was spared that decision by local Maori who regard the moreporks as taonga (treasures) and kaitiaki (ancestors), and that view was respected.

Instead Motuora Island was abandoned as a suitable shore plover habitat, and the search went on for another. A privately owned island off the North Island coast met most requirements: an area of sandspit and wave platforms suitable for feeding,

■ 'The Clears' is an area of exposed salt meadow above the southern coast of South East Island where most shore plovers live. Since stock was removed from the island in 1961, the pasture which was shore plover habitat has become overgrown. This factor plus an increase in the number of seals means the island will in the future support fewer shore plovers than now.

good nesting sites, no introduced predators, and importantly, no moreporks. Fifteen birds were initially released there in 1998.

Once safe from predators and given space to expand, plovers are ready breeders. In October and November plovers lay an average of three eggs; the females mostly incubate during a period of 30 days. Chicks are able to feed themselves as soon as they have dried out after hatching; they fledge at between 30 and 45 days. Once the juveniles have fledged, parents chase them out of their territories. Usually birds first breed at two years (on South East this is the earliest they have been recorded breeding), but in captivity and on the island where they have been released, they have bred at one year old. This probably reflects the abundant supply of food, whereas on South East there is more competition for available supplies.

Since then, 75 captive-reared birds have been released on to the island. Within two years the resident birds had begun to breed and contributed to a growing population, in addition to the annual releases. In the summer of 2003–2004 the population numbered about 50 adults, including 16 breeding pairs, which produced a record 35 chicks that season. The population is now considered to be self-sustaining, although to make sure there will be at least several more releases. The establishment of this third population is a major conservation achievement. It has helped reduce the risk of extinction should introduced predators reach the island havens.

## References

*New Zealand shore plover recovery plan*, Department of Conservation, 2001.

Aikman, Hilary, 'Attempts to establish shore plover (*Thinornis novaeseelandiae*) on Motuora Island, Hauraki Gulf', *Notornis* (1999), 46: 195–205.

# 9 Taiko
*Elusive petrel of the eastern Pacific*

| | |
|---|---|
| Scientific name | *Pterodroma magentae* |
| Popular names | taiko, tchaik, magenta petrel |
| Conservation status | protected rare endemic |
| Population | approximately 120–180 (in 2003) |
| Where found | Chatham Island |
| Life span | 50 years |
| Size | 33 cm; 460 g |
| Breeding | September–May |
| Nest sites | burrows up to 3 metres long |
| Clutch size | 1 egg |
| Feeding | squid and fish |
| Behaviour | spend most of their lives at sea; catch fish at night when nesting |

I t has all the hallmarks of a gripping detective story: in 1867 a mystery bird is shot far out at sea, then its remains end up in a museum in Italy. Almost 100 years later a young boy turns ornithological sleuth and sets out on a 34-year quest to solve a baffling puzzle, eventually tracking down his quarry – alive!

The story is that of the taiko, a petrel which is one of the rarest seabirds in the world. When, in 1867, a crewman from the Italian research boat SS *Magenta* shot it about 1280 kilometres east of the Chatham Islands, the petrel was possibly already uncommon. Hunted by Moriori for centuries (and known to them as tchaik) in a similar fashion to the titi (muttonbird) on the islands surrounding Stewart Island, the plump young were an easy target as they lay in burrows during the breeding season. However, the Moriori did not exterminate the taiko. It was likely to have been reasonably abundant until European settlers reached the Chathams in the late 1820s, followed by Maori raiders in 1835. From then it was the animal introductions – possums, cats, pigs, cattle and buff weka – which posed the greatest threat to the taiko's survival.

The scientists on board the *Magenta* had no idea where the mystery bird came from. Fortunately they preserved the specimen and it subsequently languished in the collection of the University of Turin (now consolidated in the Turin Regional Museum). It was not completely forgotten though; a painting of it was reproduced in Godman's landmark book *Monograph of Petrels* (1907–10), as *Oestrelata magentae*, later known as *Pterodroma magentae*. The species slowly disappeared from future scientific accounts.

FLEMING FAMILY

■ Sir Charles Fleming in 1938 at the Tuku, on Harry Blyth's farm, where the last taiko were known to survive. Sir Charles played a vital role in scientifically documenting Chatham's wildlife as well as advocating the preservation of islands such as South East Island.

GRAEME TAYLOR

■ The taiko is a distinctive-looking bird with a dark hooded head and white underparts.

GRAEME TAYLOR

■ A taiko with transmitter attached.

On the Chathams, folk recalled the white-breasted taiko, but as the years of the early twentieth century went by, the sightings fell away; the conclusion was that the taiko had likely gone the way of a number of other Chatham birds – into extinction. But the improbably named David Crockett was not convinced. As a young boy in the 1940s David had befriended the great scientist Dr Robert Falla, then director of the Canterbury Museum, and spent much of his spare time collecting and analysing skeletons of storm-wrecked birds collected from Christchurch beaches. Soon he was considered knowledgeable enough to evaluate skeletons for the museum, including boxes of bird bones from the Chathams. He was able to identify most, except for 11 skeletons that all appeared similar. Little did he know it, but he was on the trail of the taiko.

In 1956 a British authority on petrels, Dr William Bourne, examined the specimen in Turin. Comparing it against other petrels, and with taiko bones from middens collected in the Chathams in 1880 by H. O. Forbes, Bourne concluded that the bird in Turin had to be the taiko. Spurred on by the finding, the young Crockett determined that one day he would discover a living taiko. He was convinced that they existed on the Chathams, after hearing about farmer Harry Blyth who believed there was at least one remnant colony on his farm, on Timihonga Hill.

But it was not until 1969 that Crockett, now a senior science advisor, was able to make the 850-kilometre flight across to the Chathams. By this time Blyth had died but he had left enough clues to the possible whereabouts of the taiko. Crockett reasoned that come breeding time the birds would fly in from the sea up the Tuku-a-Tamatea River to find a nesting burrow. He spent three cold, wet, unrewarding nights in the Tuku catchment before quitting. Recalling whalers' stories of seabirds flying into tripot fires, Crockett returned the following year with a kerosene lamp to attract the birds, but to no avail.

Recognising that he would not succeed by himself, Crockett organised a seven-man expedition in 1972–73. Hidden in ferns, the volunteers broadcast taped petrel calls through speakers and shone spotlights skywards. On the sixth night of their vigil, they were rewarded with the appearance of two fast-flying birds which circled the lights for about 20 minutes. They were 'dark-bodied, white-breasted petrels that looked headless in the light', Crockett says. Frustratingly, the birds did not land.

A further three expeditions were mounted. One year two birds were sighted, and another year a team of 12 braved a cool and blustery May in wait, on the assumption that the petrel was a winter nester. Crockett, having come so far and having been so tantalisingly close to finding the taiko, was not about to give up. And finally on 1 January 1978, hypnotised by a spotlight, two weary ocean travellers fluttered to ground. The taiko

RUSSELL THOMAS

David Crockett with the first two taiko he lured down in January 1978, after 10 years of fruitless attempts to capture the rare seabirds.

# Willing workers

If any proof is needed of New Zealanders' commitment to conservation, one need only look at the taiko programme. Since 1972 when David Crockett recruited the first volunteers to help him with the taiko work, a total of 309 people have helped the project in a number of different ways – from searching for the birds, forging tracks around the Tuku Reserve or constructing the aerials needed to track the birds down.

Unlike the kakapo or kiwi, the taiko has never attracted the large sponsorship sums of the higher-profile species. That might be explained by the type of bird it is and its habits – it is at sea for the first six or seven years of its life, and when it does come ashore is nocturnal and elusive.

The project has served as a hatchery for DOC staff, says Crockett, as he reels off the names of some of those who have put in time with him on the Chathams: Dr Hugh Robertson (who is chief scientist with the kiwi recovery programme), Alison Davis (now secretary of the Taiko Trust), Hilary Aikman (in charge of Chatham Island conservation programmes), and Dr Colin Miskelly (technical services manager with DOC's Wellington conservancy).

In 2003 an assessment was made of the total amount of labour donated by those helping with the project over a 30-year time span. It came to $1.5 million. But that does not include the sponsorship dollars that have been contributed by companies such as Shell, BP and others for petrol, and hardware firms for roofing and building materials.

David Crockett is modest about his role with the taiko. 'It's not a one-man show, it's a matter of getting the right people in the right place going in the same direction and I'm lucky I've had all these people. Once they go to the Chathams and see what we're doing, they're hooked,' he says. Nevertheless, he has hunted out most of the funds and sponsorship, as well as been the pivot on which the volunteer effort has turned. He has also paid a considerable personal financial cost. Since his first visit in 1969 he has been to the islands virtually every year, sometimes three or four times a year. Each visit costs around $1500. Ruth, David's wife, accompanies him on most trips. David marked his fiftieth visit in 2004.

A typical season for the now-retired Crockett starts with a visit to the Chathams in September in order to 'get things shipshape' in the purpose-built taiko camp. Sometimes he stays through till mid-December when the first taiko arrive from the ocean to begin egg laying.

'Members of the Taiko Expeditioners and DOC personnel set up tracking stations in order to monitor the transmittered birds when they return from the sea. Three tracking stations at different locations provide bearings of the incoming taiko. The point where the bearings cross is where the birds have gone to ground,' says David. 'In the early days people used to rush off like mad to find them, but the birds used to take off again so today we're fairly circumspect.' Costing $250 each, the transmitters last between 120 and 140 days, dropping off at sea when

Personnel outside the taiko camp, October 1999. From left: Christine Hunter (volunteer), Reg Cotter (volunteer, obscured), Paul Schofield (volunteer), Graeme Taylor (DOC), Hilary Aikman (DOC), David Crockett and John Ballantyne (volunteer).

the birds moult. David wryly observes that it is impossible to retrieve the transmitters, unlike those attached to landbirds such as the kakapo or takahe.

The Taiko Trust was set up in 1997 to manage sponsorships and funds, and once it was incorporated in 2001, it was possible to apply for funds and grants. As a result, money has started to come in for projects such as a predator exclosure fence at Sweetwater, a 20-hectare area near the coast. The main Tuku Reserve backs on to Sweetwater but extends further inland. The predator exclusion fence at the adjacent Sweetwater covenant will be a boon to the young taiko that the conservation team hope to attract there – birds that have hatched over the past decade and have been at sea ever since they departed from Chatham Island. 'We're trying to track the young birds coming back after seven years; we don't want to distract the adult birds which are breeding in the upper part of the Tuku, which are so set on breeding there. We'll attract the young birds with calls and decoys,' says David.

Although most of the burrows have disappeared now, decades after the taiko last used Sweetwater for breeding, there is still some evidence of old sites. 'If we can find some of those, open them up and dig new ones and have artificial wooden burrows as well, then we should attract those birds which have hatched in the last decade. We'll perhaps shift some birds into artificial boxes. Because not every bird normally survives in the burrow, usually because of a lack of food, then we might move the ones not doing well,' he adds.

GRAEME TAYLOR

■ Tuku-a-Tamatea River in the centre of the taiko area.

had been rediscovered! Rediscovery was one thing. Rescuing the taiko from extinction would prove to be as intractable a problem. The key was to find other taiko, and their breeding burrows – a tall order in such a large area. It took a further 10 years before the first breeding burrow was discovered near a tributary of the Tuku-a-Tamatea River.

In 1982 and 1985 special transmitters were attached to the tail feathers of taiko captured at the Tuku light site in an attempt to trace their movements, the hope being they would reveal the location of burrows. The transmitters failed, but in 1987 two birds sporting transmitters flew inland to forested gullies and then disappeared into burrows which were pinpointed from the transmitters. This was the breakthrough that Crockett and the 24-member team of Taiko Expeditioners and DOC personnel had been hoping for. Nevertheless, it would be many years before the taiko could be said to have averted extinction.

# Tuku Nature Reserve

The Tuku Nature Reserve, donated by the Tuanui family, is an area of 1238 hectares, and contains most of the taiko breeding burrows that have been discovered. Until intensive trapping began in 1996, the area was infested with weka, cats, pigs, rats and possums, which endangered adult birds, chicks and eggs.

Department of Conservation seabird specialist Graeme Taylor says that despite the fact that birds were being captured and burrows found, there were few breeding pairs. That may have been because there was a sex ratio imbalance leading to a lack of female breeding partners – plus the lack of an established breeding colony

■ An historic first: this chick, hatched in January 1991, was the first chick of modern times to be seen.

had made it difficult for birds to find suitable partners,' he says. 'For me, the low point was in the mid-nineties when there was only two known breeding pairs. There were most likely other pairs not accounted for but two were all that had been found. But in the 1996–97 season we started intensively trapping predators, and since then things have improved dramatically.'

One of the first positive signs was the return of two birds in 1999 which had left as chicks years beforehand. Taiko are long-lived birds that leave the nest as four-month fledglings, then remain at sea somewhere between New Zealand and South America for six or seven years before returning to breed. Two breeding birds that David Crockett banded in 1982 were still going strong 20 years later; it is possible that taiko could live to 40–50 years, which is some insurance against extinction. David predicts an exponential increase in the taiko population over the next decade or so. By 2003 there were 13 known breeding pairs, but this number is expected to grow.

If the taiko does recover, it will probably only ever number a fraction of the original population. Professor David Lambert of Massey University has studied the DNA of the taiko and rates it to have the greatest diversity of DNA of any bird that he has worked on. What this tells us is that the skies around the Chathams must have once been thick with millions of the fabled 'lost' petrel, a scene difficult to imagine today.

## References
*Taiko recovery plan*, Department of Conservation, 2001.

# Keeping tabs on taiko

Chatham Islanders have suffered a bad press in the past when it comes to conservation. The 'last frontier', 'redneck country', 'crayfish boom and bust merchants' – the clichés pile up thick and fast. Liz and Bruce Tuanui are helping to turn that image on its head, or at least show that among some islanders there is a conservation conscience.

It's a family thing. During the 1960s, Bruce's parents Manuel and Evelyn Tuanui bought their farm off Harry Blyth, a strong believer in the existence of taiko in the Tuku catchment which formed part of the farm. Urged on by David Crockett, the elder Tuanuis set aside the Tuku Nature Reserve in 1984. Subsequently, after Manuel died and Bruce and Liz took over the farm, they themselves covenanted a further 200 hectares of land adjacent to the reserve. Neighbouring landowners Ron Seymour, Robert Holmes and Neville Day have also caught the conservation bug and are in the process of covenanting 1100 hectares of land.

Liz says she is proud of being a Chatham Islander. Her family ties to the remote islands can be traced back to one of the original farming families, the Gregory Hunts, who settled on Pitt Island in the nineteenth century. The fates of two species – the taiko and the parea – have significantly hinged on the generous donations of the Tuanui family. The turnaround in the parea's fortunes has been especially dramatic, with the population expanding from around 40 birds in 1990 to more than 200 today. 'In a way my involvement with conservation began because I was there on the spot,' says Liz. 'Things were happening on my land and it went from there. Bruce decided he wanted to protect the Awatotara and Tuku covenants because he could see the bush was receding and if we didn't do something then it wouldn't be there.'

The couple work to their strengths – Liz grows trees for planting out on Mangere Island, Pitt Island and the reserves on their farm, while Bruce does the actual planting out. But Liz makes her presence felt in other ways. Until recently she was on the Chathams Conservation Board for eight years, and now heads the recently formed Taiko Trust. 'Forming the Taiko Trust is a huge thing for us because now we have access to funding other than from DOC. Now we can really get things happening,' she enthuses.

One of the keys to making things happen is a predator exclusion fence around seven and a half hectares of Sweetwater covenant, an area donated by Liz and Bruce. Overlooking the sea, the area will be the location of a secure breeding site for the taiko. As yet, no taiko have burrows there, but the plan is to lure first-time breeders which are searching for a suitable breeding site. Some fledglings will be released from Sweetwater in the hope that they will return to what they will regard as their natal site. Finally, some breeding pairs will be placed into artificial breeding boxes and put into the reserve.

Initially the Trust had expected to be granted a percentage of the funds needed for building the fence, but in August 2003 the Lotteries Board and the Department of Conservation

■ Bruce and Liz Tuanui:
conservation is a family affair.

BILL CARTER

Biodiversity Fund provided the $270,000 needed for the job. It will keep at bay possums, rats, cats, pigs and weka. In time, the endangered Chatham Island petrel may find a home here.

The Tuanuis have other irons in the conservation fire besides the taiko and parea. Along the south-east foreshore the Chatham Island oystercatcher struggles to survive. The Department of Conservation's efforts are focused on the northern area and they do not have the resources to cover the whole island. Therefore Bruce is about to fence off an area on the foreshore against stock and predators, and is planting it in natives. Other species which the Tuanuis would like to see reintroduced to their reserves are the Chatham Island tui and the tomtit. Both were once relatively abundant on Chatham Island but have disappeared now, only to be found on some outlying islands.

Liz acknowledges that pests are an immense problem on the Chathams but is resigned to the fact that there is no simple solution. 'I'd love to get rid of cats and possums but it would take a huge amount of money and people wouldn't be prepared to lose their cats. There is not a lot to do on the island so pig hunting is a big recreation, and therefore people don't want 1080 poison used because it would kill pigs. It would also knock out the wekas, and they are an important food source,' she says.

The Tuanuis are fortunate in having children who are keen on keeping the conservation flame alive. Their son, who is at Massey University, will most likely return to run the family farm, while their daughter who is studying physiotherapy 'will do her payback for the people on the island. When the time comes they'll be prepared to take over some of the work that we've been doing,' assures Liz.

Ready as Liz is to sacrifice her time and privacy to conservation (people come and go past the house to the taiko camp), there are some activities which are off limits. Taiko spotting for one. 'I'm not keen to do that sort of work — you have to wait for a nice rainy, revolting wet night for them to come in. Anyway, the last time I went there I broke my arm. I had just got back from Canada, had jet lag, tripped, hit my head on a tree and tripped over a root.'

# *10*Takahe

## *Relict rail of the Fiordland mountains*

| | |
|---|---|
| Scientific name | *Porphyrio hochstetteri* |
| Popular names | takahe, notornis, moho |
| Conservation status | endangered endemic |
| Population | 242 (in 2004) |
| Where found | Murchison Mountains (Fiordland); Tiritiri Matangi, Kapiti, Mana, and Maud islands; Burwood Bush (near Te Anau) |
| Life span | 20 years |
| Size | 3 kg; 63 cm |
| Breeding | October–January |
| Nest sites | raised bowl made up of grasses under snow tussocks |
| Clutch size | 1–3 eggs; may re-nest up to 3 times if previous clutches unsuccessful |
| Feeding | snow tussocks or *Hypolepis* fern and rhizomes |
| Behaviour | lives in small family groups; freezes when threatened |

JANE MAXWELL

The takahe and the kakapo form an exclusive society. They are the two surviving species of birds that were once part of a guild that ruled the roost in New Zealand, before the arrival of humans. Gone are their vegetarian associates, the moa and various species of rail that have become extinct over the past 500 years.

The takahe and the kakapo cannot fly (what was the point when there was hardly anything to flee from), and they are big (because they have become supremely efficient vegetarians, and the bigger the grass eater, the better it gets at processing large amounts of food). Both are world record-beaters for size: the takahe is the largest rail in the world at up to three kilograms in weight, the kakapo the heaviest parrot at up to three-and-a-half kilograms. To achieve this weight, the takahe spends around 19 hours a day eating nutritious tussocks and other grasses or herbs.

Of the two, the takahe is the only one that has managed to remain on the mainland, having survived in the remote fortress of Fiordland's Murchison Mountains. But even here, in an area relatively inhospitable to most predators, the takahe only narrowly avoids sliding into extinction.

# TAKAHE CONSERVATION MILESTONES

**1948** Rediscovery of birds in Tunnel Burn, Murchison Mountains, Fiordland National Park

**1949** Doc Orbell initiated early deer control and stoat trapping soon after rediscovery

**1952** First takahe banded in Takahe Valley

**1956** First attempt (unsuccessful) at egg incubation under bantams at Mt Bruce

**1960** First of 23 adult birds removed from Fiordland and transferred to Mt Bruce (last removed in 1980)

**1963** Deer control intensified with NZ Forest Service taking over management of deer cullers in the Murchison Mountains

**1966** First attempt at total population census

**1972** First chick hatched at Mt Bruce from adults taken from the Murchison Mountains

**1972** Three-year investigation of regional population dynamics in three areas of the Murchison Mountains

**1976** Experimental evidence of deer preferring the same tussock species as takahe

**1976** Introduction of helicopter hunting of deer

**1978** Conference on takahe in Te Anau and publication of proceedings to mark the thirtieth

By 2004 the total population stood at 242: 141 of which live in the Murchison Mountains; 26 at the captive rearing facility at Burwood Bush; three (and possibly a few more) are in Fiordland but outside the Murchisons; 67 are on islands and five are on display at wildlife parks. Considering that there was a declining population of just 118 in 1981, the 2004 result is a triumph for conservation, even if it falls short of the magic 500 number that those involved with the programme are aiming for. In the words of botanist Dr Bill Lee: 'In my view the takahe would be extinct in the wild without the intervention of government conservation agencies, because of the small population size, mammalian impacts, and extremes of climate.'

Since 1948 when the takahe was rediscovered, these agencies have made the bird one of the most intensively studied and managed in the world, ever. However the logistical difficulties involved in researching a wild bird living in an alpine area are considerable.

Jane Maxwell knows the takahe as well as anyone. She has been studying the big bird since 1984 while she was at university; her research topic has now become her job, her official position Scientist in Charge of Research for the Takahe in

| | |
|---|---|
| **1979** | Successful artificial incubation of a takahe egg at Te Anau |
| **1980** | First birds released on offshore island (Kapiti) but later removed |
| **1981** | First total takahe population census in Fiordland |
| **1981** | First draft management plan for conservation of takahe prepared |
| **1982** | Fauna Protection Advisory Council formal acceptance of the takahe management plan |
| **1982** | Artificial incubation of eggs and captive rearing of birds initiated at Burwood Bush |
| **1982** | Widespread trapping of stoats in several catchments in the Murchison Mountains (ceased in 1990) |
| **1982** | Regular manipulation of eggs in Fiordland to ensure that each pair of takahe has one fertile egg |
| **1985** | Systematic release of adult birds initiated to establish an island population on four offshore islands over the following 10 years |
| **1987** | First release of captive-reared birds into the Glaisnock area of the Stuart Mountains |
| **1990** | Formulation of takahe recovery plan |
| **1991** | First release of captive-reared birds into the Murchison Mountains |

JANE MAXWELL

Takahe yearling. Although capable of breeding at one year old, generally takahe do not start breeding until their second year.

JANE MAXWELL

The harsh winters and springs of the early 1990s tested the resilience of the takahe, and chicks learned to cope with a snowy world.

Fiordland. When she took on the assignment in 1995, the takahe had been on the receiving end of a series of punishing winters, with numbers in the Murchison Mountains area falling to fewer than 100 birds (although there were others living on islands and elsewhere). For five of the seven winters from 1991, mean temperatures were lower than any since records began in 1973. The fall in temperatures shows a close correlation with the drop in takahe, and Jane believes the two are linked, although she points out there are numerous other issues involved in takahe management. Nevertheless, it was a difficult time to be starting a new job.

'There was a time when we had those cold winters in the nineties and when the numbers were falling. Each year when our spring survey brought disappointing totals, we consoled ourselves with the expectation that a few more birds would probably turn up in our late summer follow-up survey. But they didn't and then the next year it happened again. It was difficult to relax. But you have to learn that there are times where the environment takes control,' she says.

This was also at a time when captive-raised birds – takahe that were hatched after eggs were taken from the wild – were being released into the mountains, which in theory should have helped to boost numbers. Certainly without them numbers would have declined even more dramatically. 'We knew these birds [captive-raised] were

# The call of the wild

**The vast spaces of Fiordland have long been a magnet for romantics and adventurers seeking forgotten worlds, lost tribes, missing moose and vanished birds. Dr Geoffrey Orbell was an adventurer in the Edmund Hillary mould — modest, matter of fact and capable — who first heard of the bird they called notornis when he was a young boy growing up in Invercargill in the early 1900s. Notornis was the original scientific name given to the species (*Notornis mantelli*, later changed to *Porphyrio mantelli* and finally to *P. hochstetteri*), although Maori knew of it as either takahe or moho.**

Orbell had heard the stories told by hunters, surveyors and climbers of 'giant Pukakis which were "good eating" on the tussock tops'; he knew about the four skins displayed in museums which were the only tangible evidence for the bird's existence; and he had read accounts about birds being captured, such as that of Walter Mantell, the scientific explorer after whom the takahe was first named. Mantell records a rare gastronomic event that occurred in 1849:

> The bird was taken by some sealers who were pursuing their avocations in Dusky Bay. Perceiving the trail of a large and unknown bird on the snow with which the ground was covered, they followed the footprints till they obtained a sight of the Notornis, which their dogs instantly pursued, and after a long chase caught alive in the gully of a sound behind Resolution Island. It ran with great speed, and upon being captured uttered loud screams, and fought and struggled violently; it was kept three or four days on board the schooner and then killed, and the body roasted and ate by the crew, each partaking of the dainty, which was declared to be delicious.

Mantell was lucky enough to get his hands on the skin, which was later displayed in the British Museum. In 1851 he obtained a second skin after a Maori caught a takahe on Secretary Island in Thompson Sound in 1851. This specimen joined the first in the British Museum. A third bird was captured in 1879 on the eastern side of Lake Te Anau by a rabbiter's dog, the mounted specimen ending up in Germany's Dresden Museum. Finally, a fourth takahe was captured in 1898 by a dog owned by Jack and Doug Ross who were camping out in Middle Fiord, Lake Te Anau. This, the best preserved specimen, was mounted and displayed in Otago Museum where it remains to this day.

From that time on, until its rediscovery, no more live birds were seen. A skeleton here, anecdotes there … as a young adult roaming the mountains deerstalking, Orbell pieced together the evidence and came up with the conclusion that takahe might be living near a lake in the Murchison Mountains. Maori knew the lake as Te Wai-o-pani (Lake of the Friendless) but in 1948 it was unnamed on maps. Today it is Lake Orbell.

It was to this lake that Orbell tramped with a party of two others in April 1948. Although he did not spot a takahe, he heard an unfamiliar call, repeated twice, and came across footprints that were unlike any bird he knew.

Back in Invercargill, Orbell made plans for a further expedition in November of that year. This time a four-person team (the others were Neil McCrostie, and Rex and Joan Watson) trekked along Tunnel Burn from Lake Te Anau for three and a half hours before reaching the lake. It was here on 20 November 1948 that the supposedly extinct takahe was found.

The unexpected rediscovery sparked off intense scientific scrutiny of the takahe by leading ornithologists and botanists. Promptly the Government declared the Murchisons Mountains a 'Takahe Special Area' to which only scientists and deer cullers were granted access.

Early estimates of the population at the time of rediscovery put the numbers higher than exist today. The most extensive survey was carried out in 1966 and 1967 by the Wildlife Service, and gave a figure of between 437 and 567. Today, in the light of better knowledge about bird movements and the use of habitat, that estimate is considered too high. Nevertheless, there is no question that the population was dwindling, with numbers declining by 39 per cent between 1973 and 1982, to a low of 118 birds.

At 98, Dr Orbell remains vigorous testament to an active life pursuing his interests in the mountains. In 1998 the nonagenarian was invited to assist with the liberation of juvenile takahe into the Murchisons for a fiftieth anniversary rediscovery special.

JANE MAXWELL

■ 'We came onto the ridge suddenly and looked over – to find ourselves on the edge of a terrific precipice. Far below us a lake lay glistening in the sun, and a valley filled with snowgrass extended three miles beyond it.' – Dr Geoffrey Orbell, who rediscovered the takahe in 1948. The lake is now called Lake Orbell.

JANE MAXWELL

View across Lake Te Anau to the Murchison Mountains after a fresh winter snow fall.

good at surviving till breeding but we were not sure about their breeding success,' says Jane. It was a suitable time to review the way the programme had been managed.

Over time a three-pronged strategy had developed: the first was to maintain or improve the takahe habitat; the second was to manipulate breeding in order to make the most of the eggs that are laid each year; and the third was to kill predators such as stoats and weka.

# Habitat recovery

As soon as the takahe was rediscovered in 1948, scientists pointed out that deer were a threat to takahe because they competed for the same phosphorus-rich snow tussocks. The 1930s to the 1960s saw an explosion of deer numbers throughout New Zealand. Jane Maxwell says that in one year in the 1960s, hunters working on foot shot 1700 deer in the Murchison Mountains.

But it was not just a question of what the deer were eating, it was also how. When deer nibble at tussocks they severely retard regrowth of the plants. In experiments carried out in the 1980s which imitated the way deer graze, scientists clipped tillers of the mid-ribbed snow tussock *Chionochloa pallens*. Twenty years later these plants have not fully recovered, and it is estimated it will take them a further five to 10 years to return to full bloom. By contrast, it is believed that takahe,

A takahe strips seeds from mid-ribbed snow tussocks, a key food source. A hefty-sized herbivore, the takahe spends about 19 hours a day eating during summer, especially when it has to feed its young as well.

with their habit of dexterously pecking at individual tillers, actually encourage tussock growth.

Tussock flowering also plays a part in breeding success. In late summer takahe may feed almost exclusively on tussock seeds: 'Takahe love seeds and in good years chicks are fed mainly on these,' notes Jane. But tussocks flower only when the mean temperature the previous January and February is above 10°C; summers are often cooler than this, especially those of the early 1990s.

In 1976 helicopter hunting started and soon deer densities – at least in the grassland areas – had dropped off dramatically. Today it is estimated there are around 300 deer in the Murchisons, or one per square kilometre. Those animals are producing about 120 young a year, says Jane.

However, the numbers of deer killed dropped to about 50 a year at the end of the 1980s due to a sharp fall in the commercial value of the animals. During the early 1990s deer numbers appeared to increase slightly, and more resources have been directed at the control programme since 1997. A more planned strategy of helicopter and ground hunting to reach harvest targets has succeeded in keeping numbers lower. By 2001–2002, aerial and ground hunters were given a target of killing just over 100 deer a year, which they worked hard to achieve.

JANE MAXWELL

■ Now tussock is once more common since intensive deer culling began in the 1970s. During winter this is a useful food for takahe, if they can find the scattered plants.

Opponents of aerial hunting – chiefly recreational hunters who believe they can do a better job – point out that the reduction in deer has not been followed by an increase in takahe. Jane Maxwell counters that while on the face of it this seems correct the issue is not clear-cut. Even now, several decades after helicopter hunting cut a swathe through the deer population, the plants that takahe rely on are not fully recovered. And while deer have largely been removed from the alpine grasslands, there remains a question mark over what impact they have had, and continue to have, on the forest understorey. It is here that the takahe find sanctuary during the winters, feeding on herbs and in particular the *Hypolepis* fern.

# Egg manipulation and captive breeding

Although takahe had been hatched and reared in aviaries since 1957, the results had not been very successful. Therefore, in 1978, scientist Roger Lavers suggested that some eggs be taken from the birds in Fiordland and used for captive breeding, or 'donated' to pairs in the mountains which had infertile eggs. He argued that, since 70 per cent of wild eggs failed to produce chicks, some of these eggs should be put to good purposes.

The egg manipulation programme finally got under way in 1981, and since then every year in spring, while the snow still lies on the tussocks, Jane Maxwell and her

JANE MAXWELL

■ Takahe managers test the temperature of eggs by placing dummy eggs with temperature loggers alongside them. This helps to tell them whether the mother is keeping the egg warm enough to hatch.

Takahe on a nest under red tussock.

team shift eggs around in order to maximise productivity. 'Some areas are more productive than others. We go in for 10-day to two-week field trips in the spring. We have divided the Murchisons up into six main blocks, each of which is covered by a two-person team. They check on nests and egg quality and we then make a decision about what eggs we want to take,' says Jane.

There are guidelines on the number of eggs they can take, but there is never a fixed figure. Jane acknowledges that there is uncertainty about the effects of the programme and that is why they do not take a set amount of eggs a season: 'Because of the unknowns, the number of eggs taken varies. This year we took 16 but some years it is less. Much depends on the quality of the eggs. We also like to leave birds which are new breeders to have a go on their own rather than interfere. In 2000 we set aside a minimum disturbance area where there is no egg manipulation, so we can compare the takahe in that area with the others.'

Among the questions to be answered are: if eggs are removed and birds have to re-nest, are they put under extra stress; do pairs that are left with just one egg produce as well as those with two; what effect is continued removal of eggs having on the wild population?

The captive rearing facility at Burwood Bush, 40 kilometres east of Te Anau, is acknowledged as a world leader. At 600 metres above sea level, the 80-hectare

tussock- and forest-covered enclosure mimics the mountainous habitat that the birds will ultimately be released into. Besides hatching eggs brought down from the Murchison Mountains population, staff at the facility also hatch eggs of around half a dozen resident pairs. Once the chicks emerge, they are placed in small pens and fed using takahe puppets. This is to ensure that the chicks do not come to regard humans as their parents, and that they learn appropriate survival strategies.

All chicks get some time with adult takahe when they are very young to help them learn appropriate behaviours, and

JANE MAXWELL

■ A takahe chick just a few weeks old.

JANE MAXWELL

■ Checking a weather station in Takahe Valley, mid-winter.

sometimes puppet adults are used to avoid the chicks imprinting onto humans. At eight to 10 weeks old, groups of chicks are fostered out to adult takahe pairs which teach them feeding techniques. Especially important is the training they receive in digging for, and eating *Hypolepis* rhizomes. It appears that young takahe do not recognise *Hypolepis* – their staple winter diet in their eventual mountain home – as a food and have to be shown how to find it.

By the time the young are aged 10–12 months, it is time to be released into the wild. 'We release them into territories where we know the habitat is good, as birds have lived there in the past, but where there are no resident pairs at the time to chase them out. We usually put two – a male and female – into a territory together, or release a single bird into an area where we know a wild single bird already lives, and who could be a potential mate for the one we release. They seem to be more relaxed when they are together. There are very tight pairs, always close,' says Jane.

# Predators

As if the takahe did not have enough to cope with (high levels of infertility, damaged habitat), the threat of predation by animals such as possums, weka and stoats has to be added to the list. However, since evidence is hard to come by, it is unclear what their precise impact may be.

Possums are presumed to be a potential threat because they are known to eat

■ The one that did not get away. Although stoats may not be a major threat above the treeline, they inhabit the forested areas where the takahe seeks refuge in winter.

the eggs and chicks of other native birds such as kiwi and kokako, but there are no recorded attacks on takahe. Data on possum densities in the Murchison Mountains is scant but their numbers appear to be quite low.

Weka have been blamed for eating takahe eggs, but the evidence is circumstantial. Numbers are low in the Murchisons. At one time in the 1980s some weka were captured and moved to other locations but this has been stopped.

The chief culprits among the predators are stoats, although just how much damage they cause is difficult to say. For example, Jane Maxwell analysed the deaths of 51 young birds, finding that 23 per cent were accidents, but the causes of death for the remainder were uncertain. While stoats had visited eight per cent of the carcasses, that did not necessarily mean they were guilty of killing them. In fact, only one bird was identified as a stoat kill.

On several occasions stoats have been recorded killing adult takahe, but over the years that the birds have been observed, known attacks have been rare. For that reason, scientific opinion swung to the view that stoat predation was not having a great impact on the population. However, in the light of research on kiwi and mohua, it is now believed that predators can have a significant impact, even if their attacks are rare. This is because, in the case of the takahe, natural mortality is high and productivity is low. One estimate considers that just one death of an effective

# Island Life

**Just because the takahe was rediscovered in the Fiordland mountains, does that necessarily mean the bird is best suited to that environment? The answer to that question has helped shape the direction of present-day takahe conservation.**

During the late 1980s, some scientists, chief among them Auckland University's Professor John Craig, proposed that new populations of takahe should be established on islands, as an insurance against them becoming extinct in Fiordland. However, others argued that takahe were grassland-feeding specialists that had adapted to life in the mountains and would not fare well at lower altitudes. Explaining the fact that takahe fossil remains were found throughout New Zealand, especially in lowland areas, the scientists said the takahe had been at its most successful during the Pleistocene era (from between 10,000 and two million years ago). During that cooler period, grasslands and subalpine shrubs had been widespread and the rail had thrived. With climate warming in the past 10,000 years, forest replaced the grasslands and shrublands, reducing the areas where takahe could live.

The fossil record shows that takahe were widespread and relatively abundant throughout the country. Bird remains have been found in 137 sites, 83 in the North Island and 54 in the South. Most were discovered in caves; interestingly, only one site was above the treeline in the subalpine zone, similar to the habitat where the Fiordland population now live.

In the end the island advocates won the day. Besides the weight of scientific opinion which supported their view, they could also point to the successful introduction of nine takahe (five males and four females) to Maud Island in the Marlborough Sounds in 1984. The birds not only found exotic grasses to their taste, but they also began to breed. In 1987 and 1988, six takahe were released on Mana Island, north of Wellington, and in subsequent years further birds were introduced to Kapiti Island and Tiritiri Matangi.

The decision to put the birds on islands appears to have paid off, since it has been mainly thanks to the island populations that the takahe has increased in numbers.

And yet the island experiment has not been an unqualified success because the rate of increase of the takahe population on these islands has been slower than expected. During the debate over island introductions, some scientists had warned that island populations would not be self-sustaining because takahe would not breed if their diet was introduced pasture grasses.

This prediction has not been proved totally correct, since island takahe are clearly self-sustaining, but their breeding woes have puzzled scientists. In their intensive studies, Dr Ian Jamieson and Christine Ryan have investigated a number of factors: whether the takahe are tapping into sufficient nutrients compared to their Fiordland relatives — they are; whether aggression between males in smaller territories hampers breeding — not much more than usual; whether male and female reproductive systems are not synchronised — they do not appear to be for the first clutch but improve with the next.

Although their research is not complete, the scientists have come to the conclusion that the takahe's poor reproductive success is caused by a collision of genetics and the environment. Having been such a small population for a long time, it is suffering from 'inbreeding depression'. When shifted to islands, it encountered pasture grasslands, a habitat with which it had no evolutionary history. A test which might confirm this hypothesis is to swap eggs between Fiordland and island birds. However, a moratorium on mixing the two groups (due to possible transfer of disease) prevents this. According to Jamieson and Ryan, the best hope for the future is to select the best island breeders and thus improve productivity.

Meanwhile, Professor Craig points to additional advantages in having island populations. Besides reducing the chances of the takahe becoming extinct, island populations enable the public to become more involved in conservation. Such has been the experience of Tiritiri Matangi, an open sanctuary island visited by 20,000 people a year, where 19 takahe are now on view.

JANE MAXWELL

Takahe have thrived on islands where they have been introduced, although their breeding rates have not been as high as might be expected.

JANE MAXWELL

■ Takahe habitat, alpine summer. Nests are often located in fertile areas where the tussock is tall and the scrub offers shelter. Looking down into the McKenzie Hut basin.

breeding bird per 10 years could have a severe effect on the population.

A recent thesis by Masters student Des Smith from Otago University has helped clarify some stoat issues. His study did not investigate stoat–takahe interactions but focused simply on the ecology of stoats in the Murchison Mountains. Smith's study corroborated the findings of earlier stoat studies in other areas, that stoats are not present in high numbers during October and November when takahe are sitting on nests and most vulnerable to predation. Instead, their numbers peak in late summer and autumn, indicating this is the best time for conservation managers to be on their guard against the marauders. His key new discovery was that there are more stoats in the beech forest valley floors than in the alpine tussock zone where takahe nest in summer. This may afford the takahe some protection.

Another study on blue ducks in the lowland Clinton Valley of Fiordland, where the vulnerable ducks have been decimated by stoats, shows how fortunate takahe are to live at a higher altitude. However, as the winter snow pack forces the takahe to descend into these valley floors to find winter food and shelter, they may become more vulnerable at this time.

In a trial attempting to gauge the effect of removing some of the predators, a section of the Murchisons has been criss-crossed with a network of traps to capture stoats. Conservation managers will then compare how well adult takahe survive and how productive they are in the trapped section compared to outside.

Fortunately, armed with a strong beak and sturdy feet, takahe are not defenceless against predators, as one incident observed by Roger Lavers demonstrates. One day he heard the sound of a violent attack by an animal on a takahe pair and their chick. When he reached the spot where the incident had taken place, he discovered a decapitated stoat rather than dead takahe.

# Stuart Mountains

If the island release programme has been a success, the opposite has to be said for the attempt to create a back-up population in the Stuart Mountains, the next range north of the Murchisons. On the face of it, the Stuarts would appear to be a suitable home for takahe – in fact, they were known to have inhabited the area, more remote and untracked than the Murchisons, as recently as 1980. Therefore, once the first juveniles started to come off the 'production line' at Burwood Bush in 1987, they were released into the Stuarts. In all, between 1987 and 1992, 58 youngsters were set free. Today, based on casual observations, perhaps one or two remain. What happened?

According to Jane Maxwell, there could be a number of reasons: the quality of the habitat could be poor (there are more deer in the Stuarts than in the Murchisons);

Takahe juveniles being released into the Murchison Mountains.

A takahe yearling is fitted with a transmitter before release into the wild.

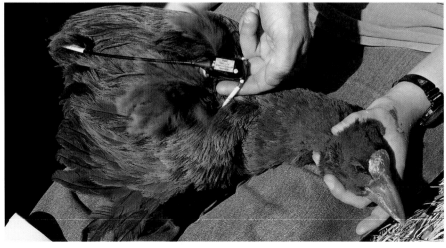

JANE MAXWELL

JANE MAXWELL

■ Playing taped calls across a takahe territory in hopes of attracting a response.

the birds had not learnt correct feeding techniques, especially how to eat *Hypolepis* fern; there might not have been enough birds released so it was difficult to find a mate in the 35,000-hectare wilderness; and because there was not a resident population, the newcomers did not have successful examples to imitate.

The trial was halted in 1993, with the focus redirected towards releasing takahe in the Murchisons and onto islands. International experts consider that an ideal number to create a self-sustaining population is between 80 and 120, and the Stuart Mountains programme was cut short before those figures were reached. Nevertheless, some of the Stuart population did go on to breed, suggesting that one day these mountains might resound to the distinctive 'coo-eet' of this magnificent rail.

Meanwhile, Jane Maxwell is focusing on improving the chances for the Murchisons takahe. It is a job she relishes. 'The island programmes have done well so you feel you've got an insurance. But the ones in Fiordland are part of a natural community. With the rigorous scientific programme we've developed, we have the confidence that we are doing the right thing,' she says.

# Beyond the Brink
## New Zealand's extinct birds

While a number of New Zealand bird species have approached the verge of extinction in recent times (but are recovering, as previous chapters demonstrate), many others are no more. Before humans arrived in New Zealand there were 245 bird species, of which 174 or 71 per cent were endemic – in other words, they existed nowhere else.

This is an extremely high proportion of endemics, but it is to be expected for such a large, remote landmass that because of its isolation for such a long time it came to resemble a continent in terms of the number of native species that evolved. Of the 245 original species, 21 per cent are now extinct.

The following is a list of the species which have become extinct since Maori landed on New Zealand shores about 700 years ago. Of these, 34 extinctions occurred after the arrival of Maori but before the arrival of Pakeha, with 15 further extinctions since.

Adzebill *Aptornis otidiformis*
Amokura (red-tailed tropic bird) *Phaethon rubricauda*
Auckland Island merganser *Mergus australis*
Blue-billed duck *Oxyura australis*
Chatham Island banded rail *Rallus dietienbachii*
Chatham Island bellbird *Anthornis melanura melanocephala*
Chatham Island duck *Pachyanas chathamica*
Chatham Island fernbird *Bowdleria rufescens*
Chatham Island rail *Rallus modestus*
Chatham Island sea-eagle *Haliaeetus australis*
De Lautour's duck *Biziura delautouri*
Dieffenbach's rail *Rallus philippensis dieffenbachii*
Eyles' harrier *Circus eylesi*
Giant Chatham Island rail *Diaphorapteryx hawkinsi*
Giant Chatham Island snipe *Coenocorypha chathamica*
Grant-Mackie's wren *Pachyplichas jagmi*
Haast's eagle (leopard eagle) *Harpagornis moorei*
Hakawai (New Zealand snipe) *Coenocorypha aucklandica*
Hodgen's rail *Gallinula hodgeni*
Huia *Heteralocha acutirostris*

Kokako (South Island) *Callaeas cinerea cinerea*, probably extinct
Kotuhi (bush wren) *Xenicus longipes*
Little Barrier snipe *Coenocorypha aucklandica barrierensis*
**Moa – 11 species**
  Coastal moa *Euryapteryx curtus*
  Crested moa *Pachyornis australis*
  Eastern moa *Emeus Crassus*
  Giant moa *Dinornis giganteus*
  Heavy-footed moa *Pachyornis elephantopus*
  Large bush moa *Dinornis novaezealandiae*
  Little bush moa *Anomalopteryx didiformis*
  Mappin's moa *Pachyornis mappini*
  Stout-legged moa, *Euryapteryx geranoides*
  Slender bush moa *Dinornis struthoides*
  Upland moa *Megalapteryx didinus*
New Zealand coot *Fulica chathamensis*
New Zealand crow *Palaeocorax moriorum*
North Island goose *Cnemiornis gracilis*
New Zealand little bittern *Ixobrychus novaezealandiae*
New Zealand owlet-nightjar *Aegotheles novaezealandiae*
New Zealand pelican *Pelecanus novaezealandiae*
New Zealand quail *Coturnix novaezelandiae novaezelandia*
New Zealand swan *Cygnus sumnerensis*
Piopio *Turnagra capensis*
Scarlett's duck *Malacorhynchus scarletti*
Snipe-rail *Capellirallus karamu*
South Island goose *Cnemiornis calcitrans*
Stephen's Island wren *Traversia lyalli*
Stewart Island snipe *Coenocorypha aucklandica iredalei*
Takahe (North Island) *Porphyrio mantelli*
Whekau (laughing owl) *Sceloglaux albifacies*
Yaldwyn's wren *Pachyplichas yaldwyni*

# Some Notable Extinct Birds

Many of the most distinctive of New Zealand's bird species were the first to go when humans, rats and dogs began to have an impact. Among them were:

## Adzebill

The massive-beaked adzebill belonged in a family all of its own (the Aptornithidae) and bears little relation to any bird living today. Weighing up to 10 kilograms, it was flightless and would have been one of the first species to disappear with Maori settlement. Many bones have been found in archaic Polynesian middens.

## Bush wren

*Xenicus longipes* was endemic to the North, South and Stewart islands. The last recorded sighting of the North Island subspecies *X. longipes stokesi was* in the Te Urewera Ranges in 1955. The South Island subspecies *X. longipes longipes* was last sighted in Nelson Lakes National Park in 1968 and the Stewart Island bush wren became extinct on Kaimohu Island in 1972.

## Haast's eagle

The largest eagle in the world, Haast's eagle is believed to have preyed on moa and other species of bird in the forests. At their heaviest, individual females would have tipped the scales at 13 kilograms, and their wingspan measured almost three metres. This fearsome sight vanished once moa and other species which made up the eagle's diet either became extinct or diminished in number. Most likely Maori hunted it too; legends spoke of how the eagle carried off men, women and children and ate them.

## Huia

The best known of New Zealand's wattle birds (the others are the still surviving North Island kokako and the saddleback, all are characterised by a fleshy wattle at the base of the bill), the huia was endemic to the southern portion of the North Island. The slender, curved bill of the female was about 105 millimetres long, almost twice as long as that of the male. It was last seen in 1907.

## Laughing owl

When the laughing owl became extinct in 1914, one of the most distinctive night-time sounds of the New Zealand forest disappeared with it. Some of the few Europeans who heard the predator described its call as 'a series of dismal shrieks frequently repeated' or 'a peculiar laughing cry, uttered with a descending scale of notes'. Weasels, ferrets or avian disease possibly accounted for its demise.

## Moa

Living relatives of now-extinct moa include emu, ostrich and kiwi, which are members of a bird group called ratites. New evidence published in 2003 has revealed that in some species of the moa – particularly the largest tall and thin Dinornithidae – the females were twice the size of the males. DNA analysis shows that some species currently recognised as distinct are probably different-sized males and females of the same species. So how did the giant birds manage to mate? Perhaps like the ostrich, where, following prolonged courtship, the female sits before the male jumps on. The last of the moa are believed to have disappeared several hundred years ago.

## Piopio

Walter Buller regarded the piopio, mistaken as a type of thrush by early colonists because it looked like one, as 'unquestionably the best of our native songsters'. Richard Henry wrote that he was regularly visited by one which ate crumbs from his plate and looked at itself in his mirror. Little wonder that such a naïve species did not last long; the last one was sighted in 1902.

## Stephen's Island wren

Three features set this small wren apart: it may have had the smallest range of any bird (180 hectares); it may have been the only perching bird unable to fly; and it was both discovered and wiped out by a lighthouse keeper's cat in 1894 on this Cook Strait island. The reason for some of the doubt is that few of the birds were observed properly before they were all killed.

# Acknowledgements

I owe a debt of thanks to the dedicated people who granted me their valuable time to talk about their work. They include Hilary Aikman, David Crockett, Jo Crofton, Alison Davis, Julie Hagelin, Euan Kennedy, Sid Marsh, Jane Maxwell, Don Merton, Peter Moore, Dave Murray, Shaun O'Connor, Ralph Powlesland, Hugh Robertson, Mark Sanders, Frances Schmechel and Graeme Taylor. A number of these people along with other contributors provided the images and reviewed the chapters.

Staff at the Department of Conservation library in Wellington were generous with their time and use of their resources.

Rebecca Lal ably steered the book through the editing and production stages and Geoff Walker was an enthusiastic champion of the concept.

Adele, Sam, Elinor and Isla Kate – thanks for being there.

# About the author

Gerard Hutching's interest in natural history was first sparked by tramps in wild places and by the enthusiasm of friends and family. He has been fortunate to make a career writing on the subject since 1984 when he became editor of *Forest & Bird* magazine. Since then he has co-produced *Forests, Fiords and Glaciers*, a book celebrating the south-west of the South Island, and written *Naturewatch New Zealand*, a guide to native wildlife. He is also the author of the best-selling *The Penguin Natural World of New Zealand*. At present he is a freelance writer in Wellington, where he lives with Adele and their three children, Sam, Elinor and Isla.

# Index

Numbers in italics denote illustrations.